ARTIFICIAL INTELLIGENCE
BUSINESS APPLICATIONS

How to Learn Applied Artificial Intelligence and Use
Data Science for Business. Includes Data Analytics,
Machine Learning for Business and Python

WILLIAM J. FORD

TABLE OF CONTENTS

INTRODUCTION

I s your marketing technique taking advantage of the significant strides in technological innovation to reach out to your clients when and where it matters? In the race of modern business, failure to concentrate on developments in emerging technologies, like artificial intelligence, can result in a level of customer engagement far behind your tech-enhanced competitors.

For years, the standard model for targeted ads has been to identify markers of behavioral similarity (e.g., subscription to a publication in a specific subject matter) and to create content that appeals your selected groups of customers.

But in today's hyper-personalized environment, this "good for the chicken, good for the gander" strategy no longer cuts. Yet the human effort required to design genuinely customized, large-scale advertising and marketing have made it almost impossible to target customers with accuracy.

Thanks to artificial intelligence, though, we now have the resources to do that, and to make it easier than ever to locate, link, and turn prospects.

Just as essential, artificial intelligence enables the streamlining of marketing systems, the lifting of prohibitive costs that once hampered attempts to improve 1:1 interactive and individualized content.

In this book, we will discuss the different ways in which companies use artificial intelligence to enhance both the quality and efficacy of their 1:1 marketing campaigns, taking a look at how AI can change the way businesses communicate with their users in the years to come.

Artificial Intelligence and why it's important for the future of your marketing.

AI is an indispensable tool that businesses can use to get important insights and cutting-edge approaches from data sources.

There's been a lot of hype about artificial intelligence (AI) recently, but few people actually know what it is. Artificial intelligence is a branch of computer science that focuses on developing software capable of learning and enhancing their performance over time. While computers are very good at quickly collecting vast volumes of data, it has historically been reserved just for the human mind to know what to do with that knowledge and information, and how to use them to achieve a specific goal.

In the 1950s, computer scientists started searching for ways to build applications that could solve problems and imitate the way people think. Recent AI systems have helped with "fast" tasks such as street mapping and, by 2003, the infrastructure that would serve as basis for cyber-helpers such as Alexa or Siri has been put in place.

Nowadays, AI's algorithms are able to constantly learn and respond to different "inputs ", whether they are human speech, x-ray pictures, or other data types. And AI's ability to change every aspect of its industry, from development to customer service, is immense.

Companies are now using AI to monitor consumer behavior, forecast population compliance, foresee sales, and provide top-class customer support. In reality, technology is now responsible for driving the day-to-day applications that we know and enjoy, like Siri, Cortana, PayPal, Google Maps, and more, across a number of AI outposts such as machine learning, deep learning, and natural language processing (NLP).

This, of course, begs the question: if AI technology is so strong, how can I use it to advance the marketing strategy of my company?

How businesses use AI to boost their marketing ROI

With the advent of AI, businesses have gained not only the potential to communicate individually with customers but also to turn the data they left behind into a blueprint for how to best represent them in the future.

As AI algorithms continue to grow, and sophisticated computing power becomes more commercially available, businesses are slowly increasing the role of artificial intelligence in their marketing strategies. Sometimes used to decode signals hidden within mountains of evidence, artificial intelligence also offers a crucial strategic advantage by offering deep statistical capabilities to accurately forecast consumer behavior.

Using predictive analytics to forecast buying trends.

Predictive analytics uses large volumes of data to forecast possible results. Companies like Target have shone the focus on predictive analytics to masterfully forecast the buying habits of customers. In 2012, the company made headlines after they were able to accurately forecast a teenager's pregnancy taking in consideration her shopping patterns before she had known that she was (unexpectedly) expecting it.

This event shows both the accuracy of the algorithms used by marketing firms and the continuing need for human control during the use of these emerging technologies.

Using deep learning to identify complex objects.

Deep learning allows a machine to "read" images, text, speech, and other data structures to save useful information. No discussion on the use of deep learning is complete without discussing how the social networking giant Facebook uses a powerful object-recognition system that uses user-submitted images from Instagram.

Although the company claims that the intelligence collected is not being used to interpret consumer behavior further, the new open-source initiative opens the door to the idea that other businesses will still exploit this analytical technology.

Using chatbots to improve customer service.

However, it is not just the cores of the electronics sector who use artificial intelligence to improve consumer service. Through the support of smart chatbots, businesses provide consumers through 1:1 intuitive, open, and interactive interactions that meet their needs and help them find valuable resources.

Last year, Shell, a global oil and gas corporation, introduced a new chatbot called "Shelly" to help consumers establish which changes are more appropriate for their vehicles.

Not only does Shelly help foster 1:1 customer engagement with the company, but, according to Mansi Madan Tripathy, Managing Director of Shell India, it eliminates downtime and decreases consumer running costs by 25-30%.

Tripathy also argued that the use of sensor-driven data aggregation by Shelly would improve both the health and operating performance of fleets that incorporate modern technologies into their company's physiology.

Bottom line:

As the prevalence of AI increases, so do the hopes of consumers that businesses can improve the level of services they offer. In the same way, as companies are supposed to offer blogs, internet ordering, and other omnichannel buying options, consumers would demand-responsive, meaningful correspondence from organizations.

Moreover, the performance of the AI literally cannot be achieved by humans. And even though we may equal the robo-brethren, the resource-intensive nature of such job benefits businesses that use the expertise of their employees for non-programmable activities.

Modern marketers need to keep considering the many directions in which AI can advance its corporate goals and then continue to implement them. Waiting to change following an industry-wide paradigm shift will leave businesses struggling to keep up.

Boost the experience of the consumer with artificial intelligence.

Companies are transforming the way consumers experience their brand, integrating clever chatbots, predictive analytics, and other customized services to have more responsive customer service.

By the end of the day, consumers would turn to businesses offering the most accessible, value-added offerings at the lowest cost. Artificial intelligence has become a crucial technology that allows businesses to satisfy not only the needs of their clients, but also their own ones.

We recently addressed how Shell uses chatbots to improve its customers experience. Now let's take a look at how Shell, or some other organization in the oil and gas business, might continue to incorporate AI into their marketing plan to better leverage anything used by most consumers at least once a week: the gas station.

Using artificial intelligence to view the data on the consumer wallet.

Many retailers are now providing consumer rewards to promote the use of brand-specific tickets, both at and off the pump. This loyalty cards provide marketers with an invaluable insight on customers actions, and the data produced by shoppers also holds the secret to predicting their potential buying habits.

Indeed, AI has already demonstrated the ability to develop strategic outlooks from programmatic data using advanced algorithms that greatly outperform previous marketing models.

In the past, consumers were targeted with ads that linked recent sales with upcoming deals (for example, people who ordered from iTunes were targeted with promotional materials for U2's latest album).

However, this latest wave of AI-driven marketing technologies enables advertisers to employ sophisticated algorithms that turn consumer buying data into measures on the individual goods they may be interested in, taking personalized targeting to a whole new level.

British Bank HSBC, in collaboration with Maritz Motivation Solutions, undertook a loyalty plan trial in which 75,000 customers were given incentive points that could be exchanged for a variety of goods and services. Some of the clients had an AI-generated incentive program, while others used traditional promotional emails.

The results confirmed the strong preference for the AI-backed recommendations. About 70% of the participants who eventually reclaimed their incentive bundle, chose the AI suggestions.

Work has shown that AI-powered predictive analytics can be used to familiarize consumers with what they desire.

Customer-friendly communications of voice recognition.

Perhaps more interestingly, voice-recognition apps augmented with mood detection can be mounted at gas station pumps, both to help consumers with their orders and to sense their emotional state.

Based on the identified emotions, gas pump screens may include drug suggestions that are ideally tailored to a specific mood. As a result, AI would encourage marketers to surpass the obstacles posed by the dissonance between their marketing strategies and the emotions of their consumers.

Likewise, voice-recognition apps can be used to speed up customer requests, allowing a smoother flow of customer traffic. Purchases may be speeded up by incorporating contactless credit cards and voice-recognition apps that will enable consumers to simply and efficiently communicate their needs to the network.

In addition, regular dialog with the AI bot (such as "Shelly") improves brand loyalty and helps customizing the company to the customer through one-on-one, customized experiences.

Support clients see a big picture with deep learning and object perception.

Let's face it: day-to-day life makes it possible to lose track of critical vehicle information, such as repairs and scheduled maintenance.

Using conveniently placed cameras instilled with object-recognition tech, gas stations may help passing drivers keep track of vital resources that they may have missed, such as repairing damaged tyres, fixing burned out headlights, or just cleaning.

However, visual interpretation should not be limited to automotive inspections. Image recognition tools may also be used to draw conclusions about consumers themselves.

In fact, the advantages of object-recognition can be leveraged to modernize the buying process inside the store. Using a proprietary app, consumers may easily take photos of things inside the shop, get those things identified automatically by the software, fit the price index and pay with the customer's credit card — without the customer ever needing to stand in line.

Amazon has already showed the virtues of this model with AmazonGo, which incorporates AI, sensor-based information, and data visualization to free consumers from the inconvenience of on-line waiting. This research helps retailers to collect more data on consumer buying patterns, to gain insight into what consumer shoppers buy, what areas of the store they first visit, and so on.

Out of sight, it no longer means out of view.

Finally, by collaborating with existing GPS-equipped apps such as Waze or Google Maps, oil marketers can track the distances that drivers have traveled since their last refueling, send alerts to the refueling station or send directions to the closest gas station at the right time. Incentives to sign in to the brand's gas — such as discounts, bundled offers, or redeemable loyalty points — can then be added to the customer's app-based wallet.

Bottom line:

Essentially, businesses will use AI to enhance nearly any part of consumer service. As Maritz Motivation Solutions and HSBC have shown, AI can be used to sift through vast amounts of data to find behavioral overlaps between consumers, including their buying habits.

Incorporating such technologies into your own marketing campaign not only increases the likelihood of a profitable sell, but it also increases the value you receive. It's simpler, more effective, more customized. So, if we've ever had that, it's a good tactic.

Strengthen your loyalty plan with your big data.

While brand loyalty programs continue to grow, AI let marketers collect valuable customer knowledge across channels.

According to Jesse Wolfersberger of Maritz Motivation Solutions, AI is a game-changing phenomenon that will become pervasive in the development of consumer loyalty programs.

Their work for HSBC's consumer loyalty program reveals that AI is able to process a far wider variety of results, much deeper and much quicker than humans could have ever achieved. Because of this, AI is able to put the loyalty system into a partnership, continuously reviewing data to provide the right deals to consumers, at a given point in time.

Wolfersberger also claims that AI's deep insight into customer behavior can help expose loyalty points to manipulation, giving marketers a valuable weapon in the battle against system abuse.

Traditional anti-fraud strategies operate in an analogous way to a tripwire in which guidelines are defined, and alarms are triggered when they are broken. Artificially sophisticated anti-fraud approaches are different: they are able to understand and build complex, developing protections against fraud, supplying consumers with up-to-date, real-time security.

Finally, the introduction of AI into the marketing plan of the company let marketers create well-honored omnichannel interactions that enable brands to establish loyalty on any possible buying site. Tarte turned everyday customers into dedicated brand ambassadors by giving redeemable points to those eager to post meaningful knowledge about the brand on their social media account.

Bottom line:

Money speaks, so do the clients. Although consumers are motivated to promote a brand because of their positive experience with the product, their loyalty is undoubtedly dictated by how much the product rewards them for their efforts. A well-engineered reward system is a fast way to inspire greater consumer engagement.

WHAT IS AI

A I incorporates a range of innovations with the goal of imitating the cycle of human thinking and rationality. The word "artificial intelligence" was invented in the late 1950s but became way more popular due to the advent of data storage, computers, and strong investment in consumer products. Late AI also tackled topics such as problem solving. Throughout the 1960s, the US Department of Defense started teaching computers to mimic simple human thought. In the 1970s, the Defense Advanced Research Projects Agency (DARPA) applied early technologies to street planning programs. In 2003, DARPA created intelligent personal assistants, long before Siri, Alexa, or Cortana became household names.

This work paved the way for the automation and systematic thinking that we see in today's technologies, including decision-making and smart search systems that can be built to support and improve human skills. AI has grown to provide multiple advantages in a number of sectors, such as hospitals, travel, security, banking, engineering, retail, and more.

The Internet of Things (IOT), a network of electronic systems linking ordinary items over the Internet, allows data to be transmitted and retrieved, and the proliferation of mobile technologies allows huge volumes of useful knowledge to be gathered. Nonetheless, searching, reviewing and interpreting the data will take a lot of time and energy to help us. The difference is that humans can only consume a small amount of information where AI can digest and analyze vast volumes of data within a fraction of time. AI adds knowledge and logic at the human level to electronic records. The next apparent technical advancement is the production of useful information, and we can concentrate on what to do with that intelligence.

The best way to look at AI is like a baby child: data is the source to experiential awareness in the technology world. A kid has to learn a range of basic skills before he or she can have a smart conversation. This child needs encouragement and instruction from a teacher; in the same way, the practitioner or specialist must always practice hand-in-hand with AI to learn how to act properly. Unlike the infant, machines have not been developed with a perceptual capacity to differentiate between visual stimuli, music, voice, scent, or touch. Nevertheless, various techniques are evolving common capabilities for the emulation of human senses. The application of these and related systems would be AI. Here are a set of primary concepts:

- Machine learning automates theoretical model construction. It uses approaches from neural networks, mathematics, operations analysis and physics to discover secret insights into data without specifically programming where to look or what to suppose.

- Rule-based machine learning (RBML) is a concept in computer science meant to include any machine learning system that discovers, learns, or creates 'rules' for processing, controlling, or implementing. For example, a rule-based system may state, "If there is a transaction costing more than USD 1,000,000, trigger a fraud check." People who developed the software should have implemented the rule into the software.

- A neural network is a type of machine learning consisting of interconnected units (like neurons) that process information by responding to external inputs and transmitting information between each unit. The method involves several data passages to find relations and to deduce significance from unknown data.

- Deep learning engages massive neural networks with several layers of processing units, taking advantage of advancements in computational resources and advanced training methods to learn complex patterns in large volumes of data. Popular implementations include image and speech recognition.

- Cognitive computing is an AI sub-field that seeks a normal, human-like experience with machines. Use AI and cognitive processing, the ultimate goal is for a computer to mimic human activities through the ability to interpret images and speech — and then to respond in a coherent manner.

- Computer vision focuses on patterns identification and deep learning to know what's in a picture or video. When robots are able to store, evaluate and comprehend pictures, they can record photos or videos in real time and view their surroundings.

- Natural Language Processing (NLP) is the computers potential to interpret, understand and produce human languages, including speech. The next level of NLP is to help people to communicate with machines using common, ordinary language to execute tasks.

- A chatbot is a software program that uses NLP and AI to mimic human communication. Essentially, this is a computer that can talk or respond to messages.

- Graphical processing units are important to AI as they have the high computational power needed for iterative processing. The teaching of neural networks needs big data plus computing resources.

- The Internet of Things produces vast volumes of data from mobile apps, such as Google Home, Ring cameras, and Alexa, but the data remains still unanalyzed. Automating AI models should encourage us to use more of them.

- Advanced algorithms have been developed and integrated in new ways to process more data, more rapidly, and at different rates. Intelligent analysis is the secret to detect and anticipate unusual phenomena, recognize dynamic structures and maximize particular scenarios.

- Application Processing Interfaces (APIs) are lightweight application bundles that make it easy to apply AI features to existing apps and software bundles. They can add face recognition technologies to security systems and Q&A functionality that explain images, generate captions and headlines, or provide fascinating images trends and in-sights.

Unlike a decision tree, the data rules are some of the fundamental guidelines for how to view or verify the data. Nonetheless, these rules or algorithms do not have the cognitive features required to view gray areas. Machine learning, or rule-based machine learn-ing, must therefore be implemented in order to continue to help it understand, without being directly told what to do. Like the human brain, the neural network is a connecting route that tends to draw data and make such decisions or hypotheses. Deep learning includes multilayer neural networks. Computer vision relies on deep learning and pattern recognition to recognize what's in a picture or video. That is what we see in face-recognition apps. NLP technology offers an ability to observe, interpret and produce human language, including speech. It is therefore the integration of all these technologies, like cognitive computing, that enables AI to have a human-like interaction with the user.

Simply put, Artificial Intelligence (AI) explains the ability of a computer to make human-like decisions on its own, and Machine Learning (ML) is the mechanism by which this is done/learned. A machine is designed to evaluate existing data and, using advanced algorithms, learn from that data if there is a statistical association that can be used to determine future outcomes.

We already use AI in a variety of ways: from Personal Digital Assistants at home (e.g. Alexa) to Social Media on your phone (e.g. LinkedIn) to Search Engines on your computer (e.g. Google).

It is a technology that has, of all, been embraced by these Silicon Valley tech pioneers and has really begun to develop itself in recent years through a number of key drivers

- Ongoing increases in the speed and cost of computer processing capacity and the rise of cloud computing;

- a huge increase in the volume of available electronic data;
- the production and use of automation

According to a recent survey undertaken by consultancy multinationals SAS and Accenture, an increasing number of less influential businesses are now beginning to explore how this emerging technology can help their goals, and most find early ventures to be successful.

The potential economic opportunities are immense and, to this end, AI is one of the four major challenges set out in the government's new industrial strategy to place the United Kingdom at the forefront of the technologies of the future.

The purpose is to ensure that the nation takes full advantage of these major global developments, enhances people's lives and prosperity, and, most importantly, it won't only come from larger enterprises.

Real traction will only be accomplished if more of the country's medium-sized businesses begin to consider how they can profit from this revolutionary trend.

Less than a decade after cracking the Nazi Enigma encryption code, helping the Allied Forces win the Second World War, mathematician Alan Turing changed history for the second time with a simple question: "Do machines think?" Turing's paper "Computing Machinery and Intellect" (1950), and his subsequent Turing Test, set the fundamental goal and concept of artificial intelligence.

At its heart, AI is a branch of computer science that seeks to address Turing's question in an affirmative way. It is an attempt to recreate or emulate human intelligence in computers.

The vast goal of artificial intelligence has led to many questions and debates. So much that no particular description of the field is universally accepted.

The major limitation of describing AI as essentially "building machines that are smart" is that it doesn't fully explain what artificial intelligence really is; Who makes the computer smart?

In their seminal textbook 'Artificial Intelligence: A Modern Approach', the writers Stuart Russell and Peter Norvig address the topic by unifying their work on the concept of intelligent agents in computers. Keeping that in mind, AI is "the study of agents acquiring environmental experiences and executing behavior." (Russel and Norvig viii) Norvig and Russell seek to discuss four different approaches that have previously characterized the field of AI:

1. Thinking humanly.
2. Think rationally.
3. Acting humanly.

4. Acting rationally.

The first two theories are about thought processes and logic, while the others are about actions. In particular, Norvig and Russell concentrate on rational agents working to obtain the best result, noting that "all the skills required for the Turing Test always allow the agent to act rationally" (Russel and Norvig).

Ford's professor of artificial intelligence and computer science at MIT, Patrick Winston, describes AI as "constraint-algorithms, revealed by symbols that endorse loop-models that tie thought, interpretation and behavior together." Although these concepts can appear vague to the average person, they help to center the subject as an area of computer science and offer a blue-description.

While addressing the crowd at Japan AI Experience in 2017, DataRobot CEO Jeremy Achin began his speech by giving the following description of how AI is used today: "AI is a computer system capable of performing tasks that normally require human intelligence... some of these artificial intelligence systems are driven by machine learning, some of them are controlled by deep learning, and some of them require human intelligence".

HOW IS AI USED?

Artificial intelligence generally falls into two broad categories:

- Narrow AI: often referred to as "poor AI", this kind of artificial intelligence works within a limited context and is a representation of human intelligence. This is always based on completing a single task exceptionally well, and although these computers can appear clever, they work with much more restrictions and limits than just the simplest human intellect.

- Artificial General Intelligence (AGI): AGI, also referred to as "Solid AI", is the kind of artificial intelligence we see in movies, including Westworld robots or Star Trek Data: The Next Generation. AGI is a computer with general knowledge, and, like a human being, it can use that knowledge to solve any problem.

Narrow Artificial Intelligence.

Narrow AI is the most positive artificial intelligence discovery to date. Focusing on performing specific tasks, Narrow AI has experienced numerous breakthroughs over the last decade that have brought "significant societal benefits and contributed to the economic vibrancy of the nation," as per "Planning for the future of Artificial Intelligence," a study released by the Obama administration in 2016.

A few examples of Narrow AI include:

- Google search.
- Image recognition software.
- Siri, Alexa and other assistants.
- Self-driving cars.
- IBM's Watson.

Machine Learning and Deep Learning.

Most of Narrow AI is driven by developments in machine learning and deep learning. Knowing the difference between artificial intelligence, machine learning, and deep learning can be frustrating. Venture capitalist Frank Chen provides a clear description of how to differentiate between them, noting: "Artificial intelligence is a collection of algorithms and knowledge that attempt and simulate human intelligence. Machine learning is among them, and deep learning is one of the few machine learning technologies." Simply put, machine learning feeds computational data and uses mathematical methods that support it. Automatic learning consists of both supervised learning (using named data sets) and unsupervised learning (using blank data sets).

Deep learning is a form of machine learning which runs signals through a biologically influenced neural network architecture. This contains a variety of opaque layers from where the data is interpreted, allowing the computer to go "deep" in its learning, making correlations, and weighting inputs for the best output.

Artificial General Intelligence.

The development of a human-level intelligence system that can be extended to any mission, is the Holy Grail for several AI researchers, but the hunt for AGI has been challenging.

The quest for a "simple algorithm for learning and behaving in any environment" (Russel and Norvig 27) is not new, but time has not eased the complexity of actually constructing a computer with a complete range of cognitive abilities.

AGI has long become a science fiction futuristic inspiration in which super-intelligent machines overpower mankind, but researchers conclude that it's not anything we need to think about now, it's too early.

AI History.

Artificial intelligence and Intelligent robots first emerged in the ancient Greek myths of antiquity. Aristotle's invention of syllogism and the use of deductive logic was a crucial moment in the pursuit of mankind to consider its own intellect. Although the origins, the past of artificial intelligence as we think of it today is less than a century old.

The origins of modern AI can be traced back to the efforts of classical philosophers to characterize human thinking as a symbolic method. But the AI sector was not formally established until 1956 at a meeting at Dartmouth College in Hanover, New Hampshire, where the word "artificial intelligence" was coined.

The MIT cognitive scientist Marvin Minsky and others who attended the conference, were highly optimistic about the future of AI. "Within a decade [...] the issue of developing 'artificial intelligence' will be significantly overcome," Minsky is quoted in the novel "AI: The Tumultuous Quest for Artificial Intelligence" (Basic Books, 1994); [Super-Intelligent Machines: 7 Autonomous Futures] but it wasn't that easy to create an artificially intelligent being. After several studies opposing success in AI, government funding and interest in the field declined – a period from 1974 to 1980 that became known as the AI Winter. Later, the field resumed in the 1980s, when the British government started funding it again partially, to cope with Japanese efforts.

The sector endured another big winter from 1987 to 1993, coinciding with the failure of the demand for some early general-purpose computers and a reduction in government funds.

Yet work began to pick up again after that, and in 1997, IBM's Deep Blue was the first machine to beat the chess champion, when it vanquished Russian Grandmaster Garry Kasparov. And in 2011, Watson's machine genius question-answer program dominated the "Jeopardy!" quiz by defeating reigning champions Brad Rutter and Ken Jennings.

This year, the talking robot 'chatbot' Eugene Goostman grabbed the headlines for tricking jurors into believing that he was a real human during the Turing test, a challenge created by British mathematician and computer scientist Alan Turing in 1950 to determine whether a machine is clever. But the achievement was controversial, with artificial intelligence experts saying that only a third of the judges were misled and pointed out that the bot was able to dodge some of the questions by pretending that it was a teenager who spoke English as a second language.

Many researchers still agree that the Turing test is not a good measure of artificial intelligence.

"The vast majority of people in AI who have been learning about it, most of the time think it's a very poor test, because it only looks at outward actions," Perlis said to Live Science. Actually, some scientists are now preparing an improved version of the study. But the area of AI has become much wider than the exploration of real, human intelligence.

Insight into AI systems

Comparison between artificial and human intelligence has been a lively debate since Turing invented thinking machines.

- Is it feasible for robots to behave like human beings?
- How far are we from the world of smart machines?
- Was the brain-inspired by the artificial neural network?

In all these and other things, the emphasis is on shaping the future of AI. Yet why don't we talk about enhancing human intelligence by looking at AI?

Human intelligence is not only about knowledge; education is also an integral part of our wisdom, and we will develop human intelligence through improved schooling. But it seems like we are much more effective in training machines than we are in training humans.

There may be a lot of potential theories for this. AI is a statistical model, and most of the time, we will create a success measure to help understand, while education has cultural, social, political, and religious elements, and the concept of help is arbitrary. In fact, in AI, we will experiment more easily in order to figure out which learning approach works better. On the other hand, there are other drawbacks (finance, time, etc.) of innovation in the area of education. Ultimately, there are comparison data sets that help people around the world assess their machine learning approaches, what a straightforward distinction is very difficult for schooling to obtain.

This doesn't mean that we are helpless. Asimov once said, "The saddest thing of life right now is that science collects knowledge faster than humanity collects wisdom." To change, let's use our AI knowledge to boost human intelligence.

Rule-based versus self-learning approach.

There are two solutions to AI; a rule-based method where you hardcode all the rules for the algorithm to obey, and a self-learning approach (i.e. machine learning) where you display the data to the algorithm and understand the patterns, the connections, the transformations themselves. There is an overwhelming consensus that machine learning is equivalent to rule-based algorithms for perceptual tasks.

Yet this is not who we are when it comes to human schooling. We're saying, dictating, enforcing the so-called facts instead of presenting the evidence allowing students to know their own facts. This stops students from internalizing their ideas. This may be enough for small problems, such as routine activities. However, in order to deal with new challenges, one has to bend and combine solutions easily. This comes only by knowing the meaning of the ideas, not by memorizing them.

The students are not called upon to know, but to memorize the contents narrated by the teacher — Paulo Freire

As we do in machine learning, we will focus on people learning for themselves, in other words, self-education.

Self-education is, I firmly believe, the only kind of real education there is. The only function of a school is to make self-education easier; failing that, it does nothing — Isaac Asimov

Stimulating Self-Learning?

Even if we believe that self-learning is the path forward, how are we going to do it? AI developers have made a tremendous effort to understand machine learning, and we have a large body of knowledge that we can dig at.

We use an optimization algorithm called gradient descent for many machine learning tasks. Basically, this is how the computer thinks. It's very easy to understand its fundamentals. It's an iterative algorithm: it solves the solution step by step. It begins with making a prediction, giving it input on how far it is from reality, making then a new, slightly improved prediction. This series continues until we are satisfied with the difference between the projections and the real facts. In other words, learning is an involved step-by-step cycle where the algorithm rethinks its conclusions at every step, developing a little more.

As you can see, gradient descent can help one understand how to do self-learning. We can also learn a few lessons by going into the testing phase.

Anyone working on ML knows by heart that you train an algorithm using one data set (called training data) and use another data set for testing (called test data) to make sure that the algorithm is not memorizing (over-fitting) but actually learning. The training data and the test data will, of course, come from the same distribution. You can't teach math and expect good answers to questions about history.

If you construct a cat classifier, for example, you train the algorithm by showing pictures of the cats Garfield, Hello Kitty, Tigger ... then you check the algorithm with various animals: Felix, Cosmo, Figaro ... If the algorithm tell that Felix is a cat, this has learned what a cat really is. If the algorithm knows that Garfield is a cat, it may have understood what a cat is, but it may also have memorized the fact that Garfield = Cat. Therefore, any professional in this area accept that we will not use training data for research. Do you think that is the case with human learning?

More often than not, when it comes to teaching our students, we prepare and test them with a particular series of questions. However, existence problems do not have predefined, static constructs. They're always changing. They can only be treated by internalizing ideas that do not memorize them. We will then approach students with open-ended questions, threaten them with ambiguity, encourage them to ponder and discover the world themselves.

Optional example: teaching derivatives?

Let's equate a rule-based approach and self-learning approach to teach derivatives to make it clear. The goal here is to show you how to promote self-learning for derivatives, not to teach derivatives.

Traditionally, derivatives are demonstrated by adding a derivative formula and explaining a variety of common functions. Students then memorize the formulas by asking a few questions. It is much like a rule-based solution to AI where you hardcode the rules that the algorithm is expected to obey.

Let's dig in an alternative way, the way of self-learning. Like we do in machine learning, the goal here is to create an atmosphere that promotes self-learning. We're not going to teach anything; students are going to know themselves.

Rapid transition is the nature of derivatives, but change happens over time, whereas a rapid is just a moment. Users will experience the inconsistency themselves in order to grasp the concept of a derivative. How do we do this?

You should open the floor for a conversation with one of Zeno's paradoxes: "Suppose you decide to hit a wall 1 meter away from you. To do that, you first need to fly halfway to get to the center (1/2 m). The same is true of the remaining gap. You must first hit the middle point (1/4 m) to fly the remaining 1/2 m. This goes on and on, and there will always be an infinitesimal space between you and the wall. You can touch the wall, but you will never reach it. In real life, we know that we can really hit the wall, let's explore what's going on here..." Ideally, this conversation can bring them to understand the concepts of infinitesimal and eternity, or at least to build a sense for them. When you don't, you'll iterate until they do, much as we do in gradient descent. Equipped with this concept, we should ask students to think about instantaneous velocity: "Average velocity is a change over a given time period. But how do you calculate the instantaneous speed? Instant means that the time interval is zero and that you can't switch because the time doesn't run. It seems that the instantaneous velocity will be 0/0=undefined. What the heck do you think of this?" Again, after several iterations (5 times would be enough:), they will possibly come to the conclusion that as the time interval reaches 0, the average velocity reaches instantaneous velocity, as we reach the wall in Zeno's paradox. In addition, this is what the derivative is (the derivative of displacement as a function of time is velocity), and they themselves reached this conclusion when trying to find answers to some questions. From this interpretation, we can also enter the above equation. I am not saying that the equations should be excluded from school, but students should consider the inspiration behind these calculations.

I am not an authority on teaching derivatives to humans. Thus, I have attempted to provide a rough description of a self-learning approach to them. What's critical here is the method, not the derivatives. This definition can be extended to any topic. For example, to teach photography, instead of setting down guidelines for good photography, you can guide students to good websites, books, etc. so that they can see and create their own interpretation of photography. In the meantime, you should arrange exhibits to exchange their pictures and develop through positive discussions.

If you're interested in studying the derivatives, watch Grant Sanderson's video. It's a perfect example of good instruction. At some point, he asks a few questions and says, "stop and think." That is the whole idea. One needs to stop and think in order to understand more.

He also says, "If it feels weird and paradoxical, fine! You're grappling with the same problem as the math fathers did..." In a way, he's encouraging you to become Newton, and that's what self-learning is. In addition, it's safe to assume that as artificial intelligence is a representation of human intellect, it would be a massive mistake if we did not make use of its results:

- we would encourage self-learning instead of rule-based learning. We realize that machine learning is the path forward for the AI domain.

- Students should strengthen their own conclusions. As we do in gradient descent, we could only be tracking the learning process, giving students input at every stage, but not the answer.

- To ensure that students strive not to memorize, we will challenge them with scenarios that have never been encountered before. For machine learning, we frequently evaluate a dataset algorithm that has never been used before.

- You would assume that these observations are already known, and the interaction between human intelligence and artificial intelligence isn't that beneficial after all. But think again, the point here is that there is almost total consensus on these observations in the AI domain, do you believe the same is true for the human intelligence domain? I do understand that humans and computers are special but different, so it cannot be assumed that the interaction is

100 per cent. It is clear, though, that there is a close connection. Let's use this important connection between human and machine learning to consider and address problems in the same way we teach our children.

HOW MACHINE LEARNING WORKS

———————○———————

The three key building blocks of the Machine Learning program are the model, the parameters, and the learner.

- The model is the device that makes predictions.
- The parameters are the variables considered by the algorithm to make predictions.
- The learner changes the parameters and the model to match the forecasts with the actual performance.

Let us draw on the analogy of beer and wine to explain how machine learning works. The machine learning model here has to determine whether a drink is beer or wine. The criteria selected are the color of the drink and the alcohol concentration. The first step is:

Know from a training package.

It means taking a sample data collection of multiple drinks for which the amount of color and alcohol is defined. Now, we need to describe the definition of each group, that is, wine and beer, in terms of the value of the parameters for each form. The model can use the definition to determine if a new drink is a wine or a beer.

You should represent the values of the 'color parameters' and 'alcohol percentages' as 'x' and 'y' respectively. Then (x, y) determines the parameters for every drink in the training results. This data collection is considered a training package. These values, when plotted on a graph, provide a prediction in the form of a line, a rectangle, or a polynomial that is ideally matched to the desired results.

The second step is the calculation of the error.

Once the model has been trained on a defined set, it needs to be checked for inconsistencies and errors. We use a new collection of data to accomplish this mission. The result of this study will be one of the four:

- True Positive: when the model determines when the situation is real.
- True Negative: where the model does not foresee the situation when it is absent.
- False Positive: when the algorithm forecasts a state when it is absent.

- False Negative: if the model does not foresee the situation while it is present.

For the sake of convenience, we have chosen only two parameters to tackle the machine learning question, namely the percentage of color and alcohol. But in fact, you're going to have to consider hundreds of parameters and a wide range of learning data to solve a machine learning problem.

- The theory that has been generated would have a lot of mistakes due to the noise. This is an unwelcome phenomenon that obscures the underlying interaction in the data set and weakens the learning cycle. There are many explanations for this disturbance to occur:
- Wide collection of training results.
- Errors in input results.
- Data labelling errors.
- Unobservable characteristics that could have an effect on the classification but are not included in the training set due to lack of evidence.

You should tolerate a certain amount of training error due to noise in order to make the theory as clear as possible.

Testing and Generalization.

While an algorithm, or theory, works well into a training set, it may fail to apply to another set of data outside the training set. It is also important to decide if the algorithm is suitable for new data. Checking with a collection of new data is the way to test this. Generalization also refers to how accurately the model forecasts the effects of a new data collection.

When we change the theory algorithm to the highest possible precision, there still may be fewer errors in the training data, but there may be more errors when analyzing new data. We're finding this underfitting. On the other hand, if the theory is too complex to match well with the outcomes of the study, it can't be generalized appropriately. That is the case of over-. In any case, the findings are fed back to train the algorithm further.

Differences between Machine Learning and Artificial Intelligence.

AI addresses more detailed problems when designing a system, utilizing areas such as cognitive science, image recognition, artificial learning, or computer neural networks. On the other hand, ML stimulates the computer to benefit and learn from the outside world. The exterior atmosphere may be anything like optical storage units, cameras, electrical parts, and others.

Artificial intelligence also allows robots and systems to perceive and perform the things that people perform. While machine learning relies on feedback received or queries asked by users. The system works by checking on information present in the knowledge base and then generates output.

The technology of Data and Machine Learning

Data science is the collection and interpretation of data generated by various sources to develop useful conclusions that will support a variety of market purposes. Data Science method includes the acquisition, purification, interpretation, and visualization of data for the purpose of identifying useful correlations and insights.

When data sets are large, and it is technically difficult for data scientists to interpret them, machine learning plays a critical role. Machine learning is the capacity of a system to learn and process data on its own, without human intervention. Specific algorithms and methods such as regression, supervised clustering, naive Bayes, and many more, are used to introduce machine learning models.

What Is Machine Learning?

We are currently living in a "data era," where a vast amount of data is collected and stored every day. To face this growing amount of data, machine learning methods have become inescapable. So much that you probably use them dozens of times a day without even noticing!

Let's start with an example of an "everyday" machine learning contribution for millions of users: the algorithm behind Facebook's News Feed. It uses machine learning to exploit users' data and feedback to personalize their feeds. If you "like" a post, or stop scrolling to read something, the algorithm learns from this and starts to populate your feed with further similar content. This learning is done continuously, and so the material suggested in your News Feed evolves with your preferences, making your user experience more enjoyable.

This is only one example! There are many others. Apple can recognize your friend's face in the photo you just took. Amazon Echo understands you and can answer your questions. Your vacuum cleaner now can even navigate its way around your house, while Netflix is recommending videos that match your profile! Machine learning has become a massive part of our daily lives, and it's not going anywhere anytime soon.

But what is machine learning exactly? What's behind these magical-looking algorithms? And how do they use data to work so well?

Formally, machine learning is the science of getting computers to realize a task without being explicitly programmed for it. In other words, the big difference between classical and machine learning algorithms lies in the way we define them.

Classical algorithms are given exact and complete rules to complete a task. Machine learning algorithms are given general guidelines that define the model, along with data. This data should contain the missing information necessary for the model to complete the task. So, a machine learning algorithm can accomplish its task when the model has been adjusted according to the data. We say that we "fit the model on the data" or that "the model has to be trained on the data."

Let's illustrate this with a simple example. Let's say we want to predict the price of a house based on its size, the size of its garden, and the number of rooms it has.

We could try to build a classical algorithm that answers this problem. This algorithm would have to take the three house features and return the predicted price based on an explicit rule. In this example, the exact house pricing formula has to be known and coded explicitly. But in practice, this formula is often not known.

On the other hand, we could build a machine learning algorithm. First, such an algorithm would define a model that can be an incomplete formula created from our limited knowledge. Then, the model would be adjusted by training on given housing price examples. In doing so, we combine a model with some data.

In general, machine learning is incredibly useful for difficult tasks when we have incomplete information or information that's too complex to be coded by hand. In these cases, we can give the information we have available to our model, and let this one "learn" the missing information that it needs by itself. The algorithm will then use statistical techniques to extract the missing knowledge directly from the data.

SUPERVISED AND UNSUPERVISED MODELS

The two main categories of machine learning techniques are supervised and unsupervised learning.

In supervised learning, we want to get a model to predict the label of data based on their features. In order to learn the mapping between features and labels, the model has to be fitted on given examples of features with their related labels. We say that "the model is trained on a labeled dataset."

Predicted labels can be numbers or categories. For example, we could build a model that predicts the price of a house, implying we would want to predict a label that's a number. In this case, we would talk about a regression model. Otherwise, we might also want to define a model that predicts a category, like "cat" or "not cat," based on given features. In this situation, we would talk about a classification model.

In unsupervised learning, we want to define a model that reveals structures in some data that are described only by their features but with no labels. For example, unsupervised learning algorithms can help answer questions like "Are there groups among my data?" or "Is there any way to simplify the description of my data?"

The model can look for different kinds of underlying structures in the data. If it tries to find groups among the data, we will talk about a clustering model. An example would be a model that divides customers of a company based on their profiles. Otherwise, if we have a model that transforms data and represents them with a smaller number of features, we would talk about a dimension reduction model. An example of this would be a model that summarizes the multiple technical characteristics of some cars into a few main indicators.

In summary, supervised learning models associate a label with each data point described by its features, whereas unsupervised learning models find structures among all the data points.

In a sense, supervised learning is similar to learning the names of fruits from a picture book: you associate the characteristics of the fruit — the features — with the names written on the page — the label. Typical examples of supervised learning algorithms are linear regression, logistic regression, support vector machines, neural networks, and so on.

Unsupervised learning, on the other hand, is like taking the same fruit picture book, analyzing all of the fruits to detect patterns, and then group them by color and size. Typical examples of unsupervised learning algorithms are k-means clustering, hierarchical clustering, principal component analysis, autoencoders, and so on.

Types of Machine Learning Algorithms

Machine Learning came a long way from a science fiction fancy to a reliable and diverse business tool that amplifies multiple elements of the business operation. Its influence on business performance may be so significant that the implementation of machine learning algorithms is required to maintain competitiveness in many fields and industries.

The implementation of machine learning into business operations is a strategic step and requires a lot of resources. Therefore, it's important to understand what do you want the ML does for your particular business and what kind of bonuses different types of ML algorithms bring to the table.

In this article, we'll cover the major types of machine learning algorithms, explain the purpose of each of them, and see what the benefits are.

Types of Machine Learning Algorithms

Supervised Machine Learning Algorithms

Supervised ML Algorithms are those that involve direct control (title) of the process. In this case, the product labels must sample the data corpus and set the strict limits under which the algorithm runs.

It is a spoon-fed type of machine learning:

- you pick what kind of knowledge output (samples) you want to "feed" an algorithm;

- what kind of outcomes you want (for example, "yes/no" or "true/false").

- From the machine's point of view, this cycle is more or less a "join line" routine.

- The primary goal is to scale the complexity of the data and to make projections of inaccessible, possible, or unknown data on the basis of the labelled one.

- Supervised machine learning involves two main processes: classification and regression.

- Classification is a method in which incoming data is classified on the basis of previous data samples, and manually trains an algorithm to classify and categorize those categories of items accordingly. The device must know how to distinguish types of content, perform an optical character, picture, or binary identification (whether the next given bit of data is compliant or non-compliant with basic criteria in the form of "yes" or "no").

- Regression is the method of defining trends and estimating the prediction of constant outcomes.

- Linear Regression;

- Logistic Regression;

- Random Forest;

- Gradient Improved Trees;

- Supporting Vector Machines (SVM);

- Neural Networks;

- Decision Trees;

- Naive Bayes;

- Closest Neighbor;

Usage examples for supervised learning algorithms

The most important areas of use for supervised learning include market estimation and pattern modeling in banking, distribution, and stock trading. In both cases, the algorithm uses input data to determine the opportunity and quantify possible outcomes.

Sales enablement systems, such as Seismic and Highspot, use this kind of algorithm to pose different potential scenarios for consideration.

The task of the supervised learning algorithm is to determine the available prices of ad spaces and their worth during the real-time bidding process, and also to maintain budget allocation within reasonable limits (for example, the price range of a particular transaction and the total budget for a certain period of time).

Unsupervised Machine Learning Algorithms.

Unsupervised Instruction is that which does not require strict supervision by the author. If the key point of supervised machine learning is that you know the outcome and need to figure out the data, then in the case of unsupervised machine learning algorithms, the expected results are unpredictable and yet to be determined.

Another major difference between these two is that supervised learning uses branded data, while unsupervised learning relies on unmarked data.

An unsupervised machine learning algorithm is used for:

- exploring the nature of the information;
- extracting useful insights;

- identifying patterns;
- applying this in order to improve performance.

Simply put, unsupervised machine learning explains knowledge by examining through and making sense of it.

Unsupervised learning algorithms use the following methods to classify the results:

- Clustering: is an analysis of the results used to divide them into relevant classes (i.e. clusters) based on their internal characteristics without sufficient awareness of category certification. Credentials are characterized by the resemblance of individual data and also by their dissimilarity to the others (which may also be used to detect anomalies).
- Reduction of dimensions: there seems to be a lot of noise in the input data. Machine learning algorithms utilize dimensional reduction to eliminate this noise when distilling the related information.
- k-means clustering;
- t-SNE (t-Distributed Stochastic Neighbor Embedding);
- PCA (Principal Component Analysis);
- Interaction law.

Using Unsupervised Learning Algorithm Examples.

Digital marketing and ad tech are the areas in which it is used to the fullest potential. In addition, this algorithm is also used to analyze customer knowledge and to change the service accordingly.

The problem is that there are a number of so-called "known unknowns" in the incoming data. The entire success of the company process relies on the ability to make use of unlabeled data and to get valuable information from it.

Modern data processing is fitted with unsupervised algorithms. Lotam and Salesforce are currently among the most popular data processing systems to implement this ML algorithm.

As such, unsupervised learning can be used to classify target user audiences on the basis of such attributes (behavioral data, personal data features, unique device settings, etc.). Moreover, it can be used to establish more effective targeting of ad content and also to recognize trends in campaign results.

Semi-supervised Computer Learning Machine.

Semi-supervised learning algorithms are the middle ground between supervised and unsupervised algorithms. In fact, the semi-supervised model incorporates certain elements of both into one element of its own.

Here is how semi-supervised algorithms work:

1. Semi-supervised machine learning algorithm uses a small range of sample data labelled to form the specifications of the process (i.e. train itself).

2. The limit results in a partially trained model that will later be given the task of marking unmarked data. The tests are called pseudo-labelled data.

3. Finally, branded and pseudo-labelled data sets are merged, producing a distinct algorithm that incorporates concise and statistical features of supervised and unsupervised learning.

Semi-supervised learning uses the grouping process to classify data objects and the clustering process to divide them into different sections.

Semi-supervised example application of machine learning

The legal and health care sectors, among others, handle online content recognition, image, and voice processing with the aid of semi-supervised algorithms.

In the case of web content processing, semi-supervised learning is extended to crawling engines and content aggregation schemes. In both cases, a wide range of marks is used to classify material and organize it in different configurations. This method, how-ever, includes human feedback for further classification.

UClassify would be a perfect example of this. The GATE (General Architecture for Text Engineering) is another well-known method in this area.

In the case of image and speech analysis, a marking algorithm is used to provide a valid image or speech analytic model with a coherent transcription based on a sample corpus. E.g., it may be an MRI or a CT scan. With a limited collection of outstanding scans, it is possible to have a cohesive model capable to detect anomalies in the images.

Reinforcing Machine Learning Algorithms.

Strengthening computing is what is generally known as machine computing artificial intelligence.

Essentially, reinforcement learning is all about the creation of a self-sustained mechanism that, during sequential sequences of attempts and failures, develops itself on the basis of a mixture of labelled data and encounters with incoming data.

Strengthened ML uses a method called exploration/exploitation. The dynamics are simple: the action takes place, the effects are measured, and the next action considers the outcomes of the first action.

Reward signals that arise while executing particular tasks are at the heart of reinforcement learning algorithms. In a way, incentive signals act as a navigation device for reinforcement algorithms. They're giving us an idea of a correct and wrong course of action.

Two main types of incentive signals are:

- A constructive reward signal facilitates the consistent execution of a specific sequence of acts.
- Negative incentive signal penalizes the success of certain tasks and encourages the algorithm to stop getting drawbacks.

However, the role of the incentive signal can vary depending on the nature of the provided information. Thus, compensation signals may be further categorized according to the requirements of the operation. Overall, the program aims to optimize positive incentives and minimize negatives.

More popular reinforcement learning algorithms include:

- Q-Learning;
- Temporal Difference (TD);
- Monte-Carlo Tree Search (MCTS);
- Asynchronous Actor-Critical Agents (A3C).

Usage Scenarios for Improved Machine Learning Algorithms.

Reinforcement Machine Learning is suitable when restricted or conflicting information are available. In this case, an algorithm may build its operating procedures on the basis of data interactions and related processes.

Modern NPCs and other video games use a lot of this form of machine learning model. Reinforcement Learning provides versatility to the AI reactions to the behavior of the player, thereby offering viable challenges. For example, the collision detection app uses this form of ML algorithm to move vehicles and people in Grand Theft Auto.

Self-driving cars often rely on improved learning algorithms. For example, if a self-driving car (e.g. Waymo) senses a road turn left - it will trigger the "change left" scenario, and so on.

The most prominent example of this variation of reinforcement learning is AlphaGo, who went head-to-head with the second-best Go player in the world and outplayed him, estimating the sequences of acts out of the current board position.

Marketing and Ad Tech processes, on the other hand, also use Reinforcement Learning. This form of machine learning algorithm can make the retargeting process much more robust and effective in providing conversion by closely adjusting to the user's behavior and contextual context.

Additionally, Reinforcement learning is used to improve and modify natural language processing (NLP) and conversation generation for chatbots to:

- Mimic the theme of an input post.
- Develop more stimulating, insightful kinds of answers.
- Find appropriate answers according to the consumer reaction.

With the advent of Google DialogFlow development, this bot was more of a UX challenge than a technological achievement.

BENEFITS OF AI IN BUSINESS

With so much hype about AI, it seems like it's the answer to all of our problems. A high tech that will do everything that needs to be done and earn the creative advantage of industry leaders. Just, how many actual benefits can you call from AI? With the number of usage cases, it is almost difficult to mention all the advantages. Let's seek to explore some of the most significant ones.

Save your time and energy.

Machines are more powerful than humans. They can work 24/7; they don't sleep, they don't need to rest, they can't get bored. This means that you can count on them to let you know about important events, even in the middle of the night; or to speak with customers at any time of the day, etc. Artificial intelligence can process large quantities of data in the blink of an eye – a job that may require hours of hard human work, and can even be difficult to achieve. AI can even take boring tasks away from people and simplify daily work.

AI is automating repetitive operations, just like automatic work machines of the industrial era. It takes a short time for AI systems to make informed decisions – more time will be required for humans anyway. This is an easy time-saver. Let's look at Deloitte's data. How much time and money can AI save the government? Data. Data.

And, what's with the money? With process management, error elimination, and AI's capabilities to improve consumer service and revenues, you can not only save time on potentially costly company operations, but also raise revenue.

Returning to the example of government labor time savings, Deloitte reports that even a small degree of commitment behind the implementation of AI could save government employees between 2 and 4 per cent of all their working hours. Medium intervention of AI and machine learning could result in savings 13 to 15 per cent of time requirements over a span of five to seven years. With good support for the introduction of AI, the future advantages are 27 to 30 per cent of time savings for a span of five to seven years.

The rising consumer turnover is one of the greatest problems that telecommunications industry is facing. Many businesses are failing to avoid attrition, often by inadequate retention methods, which are mostly focused on random contact with as many of the consumers whose contract will expire in the next few months as possible, and through offering strong discounts to others who have already cancelled their subscription. There is a lack of knowledge on which consumers are most likely to churn, and the factors that affect this harm. In our broad national telecommunications program, the goal was to reduce the churn by 2 percentage points in the section where it was the largest. During the pilot, we managed to save $39k a month to our company. We are raising the turnover by 20%, and the company ended up with a 10x return on investment.

Moreover, PWC Global reports that AI's total contribution to the economy by 2030 would be $15.7 trillion and that global GDP will be up to 14 per cent higher as a result of AI.

Generate insights into the business.

Data is often called "fresh oil" because it has been an important tool for the modern economy. Yet still big data is worthless because you can't make any use of it. Artificial intelligence can support companies with data-mining billions of data points in a moment. Whatever question you need the AI to answer, it will do it, and it's going to get easier and easier. What kind of movie is Jane going to like? Is client X going to churn? Is this thing going to sell out? AI will have reliable forecasts of possible results based on historical evidence. Artificial intelligence turns information into expertise, and also gives you insight into the future! Of course, AI is not a fortune-telling tool, but it does help the company with predictive analytics. This is a type of analysis using machine learning – algorithms use historical and current data to forecast potential outcomes.

Predictions are not only effective in the retail industry, however. For example, in banking, AI is used to forecast currency and stock price fluctuations; in health care, it is used to forecast hypoglycemic cases, for example. Interestingly, AI was also used to forecast illness outbreaks through the study of social media messages.

AI-powered systems help businesses achieve a competitive edge by developing improved goods and services targeted to their consumers, minimizing the risk of delays or interruption, lowering costs by predictive maintenance, increasing operating performance, ensuring protection and security, quickly storing data, and having deeper knowledge of their consumers.

Reduce error.

Still, artificial intelligence is not error-free. It can make mistakes, but generally speaking, it's a lot more accurate than humans. In some cases, the precision is about 99 per cent, even with very advanced devices, such as Google's LYNA (Lymph Node Assistant), which has reached 99 per cent precision and 69 per cent sensitivity in the diagnosis of metastatic breast cancer, according to VentureBeat. Artificial intelligence is not as error-prone as people are, and the main advantage is that it takes decisions dependent on availability. No thoughts, no feelings. However, it can represent people's beliefs, depending on the type of data the machine has been fed with. So, there's a bias in the machine. Techopedia describes it as follows: Computer bias is the consequence of incorrect expectations in machine learning systems. Bias represents problems related to data collection or use, where algorithms make incorrect conclusions regarding data sets, either due to human interference or due to lack of cognitive data appraisal.

Bias can occur as a result of a number of factors, beginning with how data is collected. If, for example, the data is collected through a poll distributed in a journal, we need to be mindful that the responses (information) come from the magazine's readers, which is a small group of people. The data collected in this manner does not represent the entire population.

Now, let's talk about the case of Amazon AI recruiter, who was gender-biased? How did that happen to you? Although the program only examined no image data, it also determined that male applicants were superior. Why? How? The program was qualified to evaluate the candidates by analyzing the trends in the resumes sent to the organization over a period of 10 years. Most of the resumes came from guys, since they typically dominate tech roles.

However, even with this kind of errors arising once in a while, artificial intelligence is still less biased than humans, being then more reliable. The good thing is, even if the program makes a mistake, it can be corrected. It's not that easy with a real human, on the other hand. How do you change someone's mind on gender or racial equality? The question of computer bias is sometimes raised as a justification not to incorporate artificial intelligence. However, no human being can be as accurate as artificial intelligence. It is always worth noting that the prejudice of AI is the product of human mistake or judgment.

Enhance the experience of the client.

Artificial intelligence technologies support both companies and their customers. It's much easier to explain the compilation of various forms of data when you actually add interest. Many users are well aware of how many information corporations like Google or Twitter are gathering from them; but in exchange, we get what's considered a "free" service. In fact, it is "free" in terms of monetary payment, however, our personal details are the currency we use to pay for these services. So, are we really all right with that?

People value the fact that Netflix sends them videos that are genuinely interesting, Spotify makes custom playlists that they like, Uber comes instantly and takes them to their destination at a reasonable price, Alexa plans their shopping list. They know where we work, what our jobs are, where we are at the best time of the day, what we do, what we watch, what we listen to. Through studying consumers actions, marketers may guarantee that the goods or services they sell are useful and appealing. They're creating unique interactions. And frankly, personalized services in the past have become a privilege that only the richest could afford. Nowadays, however, the overwhelming amount of data generates correlations that allow companies to know about consumers and be prepared to handle them differently.

Another important thing is that AI is available non-stop. AI-powered devices can support consumers no matter the time of day. In the transport sector, AI is used to connect with customers real-time to send customized travel information and to provide them with up-to-date information about their transit, e.g. where they are, or when they should arrive at their destination.

At a time when the market is extremely competitive, AI-powered technologies help create great customer service to improve their loyalty and boost sales. Research by Zendesk reveals that 42 per cent of B2C consumers shop more after a positive customer service experience, while poor customer service experiences result in

52 per cent of consumers not purchasing. 59 per cent of shoppers who have witnessed personalization believe that they have a major impact on their purchasing decisions. When Amazon launched the recommendation system, sales increased by 29 per cent. Such numbers show that the "everyday" use of AI that consumers are already used to, brings real value.

Advantages of AI – unlimited?

As you can see, all of the advantages abovementioned are very common. What is it? Well, in fact, every use case brings different benefits. Artificial intelligence can boost customer experience through the use of chatbots and recommendation systems, raise sales through recognition and max.

WHAT BUSINESS LEADERS NEED TO KNOW ABOUT AI

Problems will begin with how we interpret "AI" and related words for business audiences. If you follow the most popular Artificial Intelligence posts, it's easy to get swept up in their thought-provoking consequences and forecasts. The effect of AI on culture and everyday life should be felt by all, and many journalists and futurologists will help us deal with what that involves.

Company is more prosaic, though, and what is most relevant typically comes down to sales, expenses, consumers and competitiveness. Clearly, there is a need to address larger image concerns, even legal ones. But also, these are heavily affected by the same four goals in the company sense.

So, to understand what AI means to business leaders, we should continue by looking at the topic through the kind of lens they use. What quickly becomes apparent is that even clarifying what the word "Artificial Intelligence" entails to a company audience is not as easy as we would have expected.

There are several meanings, each of which meets the interests of various viewers. Some concentrate on computer science, while others show the past of the word. Some are very philosophic in nature; others are of doubtful utility.

For instance, one of the top five search results for "What is Artificial Intelligence" told us that "Artificial Intelligence, also called Machine Intelligence, is machine-proven intelligence." We are exacerbating this by using 'AI' as a catch-all suffix for a variety of related (-ish) concepts, such as Artificial Intelligence, Machine Learning, Deep Learning and Big Data. There are, of course, major differences between them, but they are not relevant here. For our purposes, we will use a single mark ("AI") and describe it in business-oriented terms. Business customers typically tend to concentrate on actions, results and market interest. So to frame the discussion for business audiences, here is the definition of AI that we use at 'AI Prescience': for business, "AI" means computer- that perform, improve or reshape business activities by simulating human behavior, with the goal of enhancing business efficiency, or efficiency At one level, this is a fairly straightforward view of AI, with an emphasis on business outcomes.

Note, however, that the distinguishing characteristic of AI is its capacity to mimic human behavior, not to reproduce it. That is not necessarily what we think, because it means that how simulation is done is subordinate to what it facilitates. Yet that's usually the truth for companies.

Why Business Leaders Do Not Know If AI is "Intelligent"

This kind of connotation is taken away from the fact that — in a business context — it is not relevant if artificial intelligence functions the same way as a human brain. It doesn't matter whether or not AI is "truly" intelligent.

What matters to business is whether AI can produce better results in jobs where human beings are/were needed. This view sees AI as just another step in the evolution of computerization, and even industrialization. What sets this step apart from earlier technology is that it carries out (and gradually improves) things that we thought only humans could do.

This is because it consists of computational programs with features that we thought were reserved for humans. Examples of human characteristics AI simulates include:

- Understanding and recognition of our environs (such as cameras in self-)
- Interpreting and assigning "meanings" to information (such as converting hand- sketches and notes to HTML web pages)

- Handling ambiguity (such as knowing whether someone looking online for "golf clubs" wants to buy golf equipment or find places to play). Now, we've got a chance to simplify any or all of it. If the result is stronger, whether the intelligence is "actual" or artificial is not especially important in terms of market results.

That's not to suggest that business leaders should not be involved in the other ramifications of AI, such as ethical dilemmas and the effect on the workplace. Or, if anything, the reverse. It's just that if their decision-making standard is solely market results, potentially complicated AI decisions can then seem very straightforward. But that's going to push us through a very different debate, one after another.

For the time being, the biggest message for market executives is that AI development in the industry is more about changing the things that people historically had to do.

But that's just scratching the surface, of course. What else company leaders need to learn about AI?

Why should Market Leaders take note that AI is all about data & computation?

When market owners have an insight on what AI is, they generally don't need to grasp the nuances of how it functions. However, the understanding is not complete without the knowledge of some of the fundamental principles.

Of the main concepts behind AI, perhaps fundamental to business is that AI requires powerful machines to store huge, unprecedented volumes of data. Irrespective of implementation and intent, AI is basically searching for trends, correlations and variations in the data it receives.

The consequences for market audiences are: to benefit from AI, and companies need to collect and maintain large volumes of data, use extensive computer analysis, storage and resources to derive value from it. It could entail new capabilities, which were not historically applicable to most companies.

The data we are concerned about is not just conventional computerized company records, such as sales receipts, product catalogues and customer account descriptions; but it also contains printed records, web material, handwritten pages and audio-visual materials (e.g. photographs, videos and phone calls).

That's because today's technologies can digitally collect almost all meaningful details, regardless of what type, almost. With previous waves of technology, data could generally only be inserted into a computer system.

One way to bring this to life is to ask whether a person can identify a piece of data and understand what it means. If they do, so either AI can, or eventually it can learn how to do it. So, it's definitely going to be able to do so quicker, to accommodate even bigger volumes.

Company data sizes are mind-boggling — hundreds of millions or billions of things (such as bank transfers or consumer electronic clicks and scrolls) are commonplace.

Yet cheap storage means that we can conveniently store all of this and more. And cheap computational power means that we can easily scan the details. And, from a certain point of view, it makes sense to archive everything we might possibly learn about a market operation, in case it happens to be useful.

That's why cloud computing is always linked to AI. Most of what AI can do for the industry today has been technically feasible before as well, but with prohibitive costs or timescales. Today, it's inexpensive and convenient for everyone to use computing resources that were traditionally only available to governments and large businesses.

So, to use AI efficiently in your business, you may need to collect and process data volumes that you may not have previously taken care of, and use technologies that you may not have previously considered appropriate.

And to do so, you're going to need access to the resources you may not have wanted before.

How AI Skills Unleash Data & Computing Combined Strength

AI teams are developing applications that integrate data and computation in two specific ways.

One collection of AI technologies turns collected data into accessible knowledge to be passed on to other programs (AI and non-AI) to do something useful with it. Examples:

- Recognizing text in photographs or handwriting details.
- Recognizing words in details that consist of spoken commands or records.
- The detection of facial expressions in data, consisting of videos and images.
- The second form of AI technology analyzes the data gathered in order to identify trends, correlations and anomalies. They are used to notify company decisions or actions.
- AI can, for example, analyze sales data to discover new, or previously unseen, insights into what makes a company successful with individual customers.
- If an obstacle is met by a self-driven fork-lift vehicle, AI can make it idle and re-route to its destination with the least delay. If the challenge is a vulnerable human, he or she will call for help.

Well using AI in business means using these technologies to solve real, relevant business problems. AI experts will be familiar with the features of the problem, and that make it ideal for an AI solution.

The most apparent example of such a function is the availability of adequate volumes of accurate data. But there are also other characteristics of the problem that make it (or not) ideal for an AI solution.

AI programs also need to learn from something in order to address a business problem — usually enough examples of right and wrong solutions to find out what to do with a new case. However, it might also be possible to come up with a series of rules to implement the AI system.

How an AI system thinks, is educated and deals with unpredictable circumstances is a vital part to develop AI systems. That is also when variations in vocabulary tend to exist, with terms such as "supervised" and "unsupervised" schooling, or "narrow" and "general" knowledge emerging.

One of the essential things about AI to consider, for business leaders, is to pick the right challenge to tackle and the right market change to the goal. This will largely rely on the expertise of their AI staff, along with restrictions such as scheduling and budget.

Yet hopefully, it's going to be important where business executives have a degree of awareness about themselves. This is because applying AI to the industry is a real minefield of unpredictable outcomes and unintended effects. There appear to be a growing array of instances where corporate executives pay the price for high-profile IT problems, not technology executives.

And, if AI's business outcomes are not good, the blame lies with the business leaders who ordered the research, not the data scientists who did it.

Data Holds Secrets About Our Industry & Consumers We're not likely to know yet.

The more data we have on company organizations such as consumers and goods, the more relationships AI can examine between them.

E.g., if you know the customer name, address, date of birth and transaction history, you can start creating some valuable insights. Even if you do learn more about their daily life, how they spend their spare time, and how they have the most effect over them, there are more valuable information to discover about them.

Retailers have done this for years, e.g. using age, class, socio-economic background, and so on, for targeted promotions. But now, we have access to more data than we ever imagined we could. For example, social media accounts and updates together offer a nuanced picture of a person's personal and professional life.

AI provides the opportunity to access the secrets kept inside the records, in ways that business is only beginning to understand. More specifically, we're only beginning to understand what our data should express, and the kind of inferences and theories that arise.

This also happens because of unexpected effects and is usually understood only through reconsideration. For example, high profile problems surrounding unintended ethnic or gender discrimination of recruiting processes indicate that diversity is going to remain a controversial feature of AI for a long time to come.

Another explanation begins with the ad placement, then finishes somewhere that we obviously haven't seen yet:

- It's normal to get a little frightened when an online ad "knows" about the website you've just visited, maybe with another application.
- It's even more disturbing when a commercial refers to something you mentioned in an email or social network post.
- If businesses know so much about you that they can pick hyper- advertisements, who will decide what else they

could/would/should do with that knowledge as they discover new ways to monetize it?

When things are set up, the solutions are undoubtedly those of the corporate executives of these organizations. So, they're there.

Takeaways to the company executives.

- In order to make successful use of AI in your business, you need a wide variety of data of different types.
- You would now require more computing resources and capacity than you previously had before and new expertise of those on the existing technology & company teams.
- The more data you get, the more ways you're going to figure out how to use it.
- As the forms you can use data & AI through, so will the chances to make & save money.
- But that would go hand-in-hand with expanded incentives to do illegal stuff with data and AI technology — unintentionally or knowingly.
- Efficient use of AI technologies to enhance business is a joint endeavor because as a market leader, you are part of a large team of people who will make progress.
- However, when AI creates issues, liability can be less broadly spread.

- As a market executive, you are part of a much smaller community who can decide how a company plans and reacts to AI's business opportunities and threats.
- And as regulators and policymakers generally fail to keep up with technological advances, you may find yourself facing concerns, decisions and dilemmas far beyond your own business.

AI MODELS AND NETWORKS

How to build AI strategies for your business

While much is understood about developing a market plan, the development of an AI plan is a new area. How do you approach the development of your AI strategy?

Artificial Intelligence holds great opportunities across markets and sectors. Andrew Ng, the world's leading AI Evangelists, mentions the development of an AI plan as a key element of his AI Conversion Playbook. With AI set to turn every sector, how do you put in place a sensible strategy to use its power? How exactly is the AI strategy? What are the gaps in the design of an AI strategy for startups vs. corporations?

The development of the AI strategy is different from the design of a conventional one. The goal of this chapter is to lead clinicians through the process of developing a tailored AI plan. The findings are based on my personal experience and professional conversations with top AI experts from organizations, including Toyota,

Google, AI Fund, and many others. You will learn how the AI strategy applies to the company plan, its key elements, and how to distinguish a positive and a bad AI strategy.

The Business Strategy and the AI Strategy.

There is an AI approach to help the business strategy. The business plan determines the path forward for your company. What programs will have the greatest business value? What features distinguish the product from its competitors? Business strategy is articulated by tangible goals, e.g., in the form of Key Performance Indicators (KPIs) or Objectives and Key Results (OKRs). Such approaches monitor progress towards achieving the goal of the AI strategy. Raphael Kohler, Vice-Chairman of the German Chinese Association of AI, notes that it is important to have a good understanding of the purpose of the AI strategy. He points out that the debate can not be based on technology, but must be guided by business value.

There is no one-size-fits-all for the AI approach as for the business strategy. — Dominik Haitz.

The corporation aligns with the satisfaction of these KPIs. The AI strategy's goal is to provide a roadmap for the KPIs to be effective.

Opportunities and Challenges of AI.

Balancing AI's strengths and weaknesses are key to understanding how AI can help your business strategy.

You can't expect to get anything useful by telling the wizards to sprinkle the machine learning magic on your company without any initiative from you first. — Cassie Kozyrkov.

Generally speaking, AI can do three things: simplify operations, create new goods, improve existing products. An example of automated processes is Robotic Process Automation, which frees workers from tiresome, repetitive tasks. AI will also help businesses to develop entirely new goods, e.g., smart home speakers are powered by AI. Finally, it can also boost current goods. The bulk of credit assessments today are driven by AI. The algorithm is crunching even more knowledge than humans do, thereby reducing the total cost of consumer credit.

Moreover, AI is dealing with complicated tasks that require context comprehension, or something that a person requires to do more than once. AI is very good at executing narrowly defined activities and performs less well in unpredictable conditions.

It is important to consider the nature and limits of AI before preparing AI efforts.

Leverage AI to build an edge that is unique to the business. — Andrew Ng, guy.

Now that you understand how the AI strategy applies to the company strategy and what possibilities and problems arise, how do you approach the development of one?

The key elements of the AI approach

Much like every company has been impacted by energy, every company would be, one day, impacted by the influence of AI. Although no AI strategy is the same, they all need to address similar questions. The central components of every AI approach include the Holy Trinity: Data, Infrastructure, Algorithms, surrounded by the foundations of Skills and Organization. Let's dig into each of the components.

Data.

There can be no AI without data. They refer to all pieces of information that are important to the development of the company. It can be everything from self-driving car sensor data to financial data for business decisions. The implementation of data policy is a critical part of every AI approach. Andrew Ng advises that the following questions should be addressed:

- What data can you strategically collect?
- Are you gathering all or selected data?

Jason Risch, AI Director at the AI Company, stresses the importance of the pace of strategic data acquisition. Data drowsiness should no longer be an option. Jason observed the collapse of "select" data approaches in both startups and companies. Startups that concentrate on a design before developing a functional company lose precious capital. Similarly, businesses that buy startups because of their abundance of data frequently struggle to see interest in them. This is a typical weakness in the health care industry, where businesses are betting that computers will find a trend in random results. The trick is to collect "right" info.

Data is the main source of corporation ascensions in the past decade. Data-driven decisions are the key to success, so you need to identify a strong data strategy. - Tarry Singh.

After developing a data plan, it's time to talk about the next step.

Infrastructure.

It is the second main aspect of the AI approach. Infrastructure is concerned with making the data available and providing the necessary computing power to process the data. AI models are thirsty for computing resources, and the AI team needs the right infrastructure to build and deploy models. Ideally, this network is customized to the needs of the businesses.

- Could you set up a single data warehouse?

- Do you use cloud infrastructure or on-site solutions?

The centralized data warehouse centralizes access to the data available in the organization. In conventional businesses, you can find data stored in silos that can not be viewed by other departments. This also has economic, corporate, and legal foundations. However, building correlations through business-team-specific data is at the core of your AI work. Data Scientists specialize at discovering trends at data, and the goal is to give them access to as much data as possible.

The key question is whether you depend on cloud providers or develop your own AI network. Software providers like AWS, Microsoft, or Google are selling out-of-the-box AI applications. You only pay for what you use, while you use it. There are also vast amounts of tools available to help you set up fast. You must spend time and money to manage the servers. You have higher operating expenses when you purchase your own equipment. Cloud platforms are easier to start with, but, in the long run, it will pay off investing in your own network. Pros and cons rely on the business, so it's important to learn the needs before you make a decision. Tarry Singh, CEO, and Co-Founder at deepkapha.ai, does not advocate relying exclusively on the cloud for businesses building algorithms as a strategic edge.

If you learn how to use AI hardware, find the algorithmic component.

Algorithms.

Algorithms are at the top of AI's holy trinity because they use data and infrastructure to churn out valuable products. The algorithmic part of your AI strategy is tricky. Answering these questions will get you further.

- Are proprietary algorithms a key driver of business value?
- Do you open-source your models or prefer to keep them proprietary?

Cassie Kozyrkov, Chief Decision Scientist at Google, reckons that two worlds of Machine Learning exist: Machine Learning Research and Applied Machine Learning. Conducting research requires a different approach than applying existing algorithms.

The AI community has become much better at releasing public data sets and models that can be reused. This provides a tremendous advantage to your company because you have access to the variety of the AI Model Zoo. The main question you should answer in your AI Strategy is if algorithms are the main business driver for AI functions. If yes, you should set up a patent program and incentivize employees to file for patents. If not, you should consider to open-source your models, leveraging crowd knowledge to improve your algorithms.

Next, let's look at the skills needed to utilize AI in your company.

Skills.

Once the holy trinity of AI is in place, you need people to fulfil its destiny. People are at the core of putting your data, infrastructure, and algorithms to work to generate business value. How do you empower the people in your organization to use AI? Answer the following questions in your AI Strategy:

- Do you build an in-house team, or do you outsource tasks?
- How do you continually educate management and employees about AI?

Andrew Ng recommends building an in-house AI team. AI feeds off domain knowledge, and that can be hard to outsource. Outside consultants likely don't know your data, infrastructure, and problems as well as your own employees. Hence, the feasible way is to bundle enthusiastic employees and educate them about AI.

Dominik Haitz, Data Scientist at 1&1 Ionos, states that AI as a novel technology differs from other tech innovations. People are often not only unaware of AI's actual capabilities, but also, they frequently have misconceptions about it. This can range from 'omnipotent threat to humanity' to the notion of a multipurpose system that works straightforwardly out of the box.

Once the in-house team is in place, they need to act as an enabler. The promises of AI are too vast to encapsulate them in a single team. The AI Strategy should implement a program that continually educates all people to look for AI use-cases. Very often, these programs should target high-impact individuals who can invest in AI projects. Rachel Berryman, Co-Founder of todoku.ai, is convinced that managers understanding of AI is crucial, as it will trickle down as AI opportunities to employees in their line.

Let's investigate the final component of your AI Strategy — the organization.

Organization.

The last but arguably most important component of the AI Strategy is to prepare your organization for AI. Evaluate precisely your organizational design and the development processes. Then, align them with best practices.

- How do you enable your AI team to provide business value across teams and domains?
- Are your processes ready for the ML workflow?

The benefits of Artificial Intelligence are omnipotent; it is paramount to understand that AI cannot work in silos. Instead of working in vertical customer-focused business units, AI can be seen as a horizontal enabler of the company. AI is capable of impacting internal processes, create new products, or improve existing ones. To do that, Andrew Ng recommends establishing a separate unit which becomes the central enabling point of AI across the company. This unit then works together with existing departments to find high-impact AI projects and to support their implementation.

Enabling AI across the company requires understanding of the Machine Learning Workflow. This follows a highly iterative process, with the outcome far from certain. You can use tools like the AI Project Canvas to evaluate the potential for success, but you can hardly guarantee specific outcomes. The very experimental nature of AI makes it hard to follow company-wide goal measurements.

You can't promise a working model without thoroughly evaluating the data. Thus, it is difficult to estimate the real business impact of AI projects without first investing in ETL and initial data analysis. — Rachel Berryman.

Consider your processes: are they ready to support AI? If you work in a safety-critical industry, chances are that don't exist processes to verify statistical learning models. Does your company follow waterfall engineering processes? Reconsider your current development process and check if it aligns with the Machine Learning Workflow.

Now that you understand the fundamental components of an AI Strategy let's have a look at how to avoid common pitfalls.

THE PLANNING UNIT
OF THE AI

The development of an AI plan is a team effort. You need a range of insights around the key elements of the AI approach. The team composition varies among entrepreneurs and businesses. Startups build an AI approach in smaller teams based on technical input from the Software Engineer and market input from the Product Owner or Business Manager. Corporate departments have more functionalities. Andreas Meier, who has developed an internal AI approach for the world's largest carmaker, understands that in organizations with specific positions, you need a lot of market experience in order to pursue a successful AI approach. You need a wide number of people with specific positions in a company, while in companies you can build a marvelous AI approach with a few generalists.

Hallmarks of right and wrong AI Strategies

Across firms, right and wrong AI tactics share similar character-istics. Effective AI Plans are impact-driven, well-funded in the business and well-funded in terms of time, compensation as well as aspirations. Bad AI Approaches are hype-driven, concentrate on technology over effects, and hire 2–3 Data Scientists working on projects. Make sure you seek to get away from the latter.

AI Strategies for businesses and startups

Creating an AI approach is specific for businesses and startups. Raphael Kohler states that companies need to accept outdated processes and are often confronted by the change management of the current enterprise, while startups should rely on joining the virtuous AI loop. Andreas Meier recognizes that it can be difficult to map out an impact course for AI. He notes that there is a great deal of room in big companies in order to simplify AI processes. To Andreas, it's essential to start and deliver value.

On the other hand, companies will concentrate on producing a product that performs well without AI but grows slowly as more consumers use the product. Customer interactions are then eval-uated in order to enhance the commodity, thereby drawing more and more consumers. If they have joined the AI virtuous loop, AI startups are certainly on the road to success.

Information is the oil that fuels the AI engine, so it cannot be understated how necessary it is to learn about how to collect the original collection as well as the correct input from consumers to develop the product iteratively. —Jason Risch How to develop Machine Learning Models.

In order to build a good machine learning model, you need to follow a few steps:

- Formulate the problem.
- Collect and clean up the data.
- Visualize the results.
- Prepare the algorithm.
- Assess the outcome on the basis of the specifications.

You're going to take these steps to solve the problem: formulate a query.

The problem is the same one you've seen before, despite the film budget and revenue. The problem is, "How much money/revenue is the film going to make?" You need to gather your info.

In order to do a data review, you need a film budget in USD and a film income in USD. You might use this website to collect your info. All you need to do is import the data and open it for your analysis in Excel format. (To make things simpler, you can also import the data from here.) Clean the data.

The next move is to clean up the wrong details. You may have found that, in certain situations, the data in the Excel sheet contains $0.

The explanation for this may be that the dates of the movie are in the future, or that the movie never came out. There could be even more reasons to include a $0 number in it, but for now, delete these $0 rows. This way, they don't cause any false errors in the experiment and concentrate on those of actual outcomes.

As discussed above, the emphasis will be on the two columns of the output budget and the world total, since these are the columns that you will map on the graph. After the data is cleared, delete the $sign and replace the name of the section.

Explore and Visualize.

It's time to see if the production budget and the world gross are connected to each other. Now, in order to do this, import the.csv file so that you can do some magic on it. Click on the Jupyter logo for this, and it will take you to the computer. Click Import to import a file called Movie_Revenue_Edited.csv.

The next move would be to begin with a new notebook. Go to File Menu- > New Notebook- > Python 3 in the Jupyter file. This will open a new Python notebook instance for you. I've changed my journal to My Movie Prediction. (You can also view the full

Film Linear Regression Notebook). At this point, you need to use the Pandas application to access the csv file in your notebook. Pandas is a pre-built data science library that helps you to easily analyze as well as clean up results. It's built on the top of the popular data science library named NumPy. Pandas work on a wide range of data sets, such as Excel, CSV, SQL. You may write either a markup or a code in each cell. You should pick a code cell and then run it to get the results correct on the notebook.

Here is an example of importing the file and showing the data (be sure to insert the code in the individual cells as seen in the image):

import pandas as pd

#read csv file into data using pandas read_csv method

data = pd.read_csv('Movie_Revenue_Edited.csv')

data

The next step is to load the data into the X-axis and the Y-axis for the map. X will be the production budget, and Y will represent the global gross of the datasheet. To serve this function, you will need to map the csv data into rows and columns. This can easily be done by using the Pandas Data Base. Data Frames is a two-dimensional and heterogeneous tabular data structure with defined axes, i.e. rows and columns. The data frame package needs to be imported before using it in the code, which is somewhat close to the way you upload packages in JAVA and C#. Go back to the cell in which you imported the Pandas Library and add the latest one from the side after the code has been inserted and then run the cell again.

import pandas as pd

from pandas import DataFrame as df

```
In [5]: import pandas as pd
        from pandas import DataFrame as df
```

Now, in order to have the data loaded onto the X and Y axes, you must load the production_budget data frame and the Y-axis with the worldwide gross data frame. Make sure that you have the same name for the column you entered in the csv info. The application is going to look like this:

X = df(data, columns=['production_budget'])

Y = df(data, columns=['worldwide_gross'])

```
In [4]: X = df(data, columns=['production_budget'])
        Y = df(data, columns=['worldwide_gross'])
```

Since you've successfully extracted the data, you can now visualize it. In order to do so, you will need to load another module referred to as Matplotlib. It has a large library of graphics and plotting features. The pyplot function will be included in this section. For import, the right element, just add the import statement. Make sure you press the Run button every time you write a new file to execute a cell file.

import pandas as pd

from pandas import DataFrame as df

import matplotlib.pyplot as mp

```
In [9]: import pandas as pd
        from pandas import DataFrame as df
        import matplotlib.pyplot as mp
```

You'll write a code to print a plot in a new cell. You'll use Scatter Plots here to help you identify the connection between these two variables. You need to use the pyplot.show() method to represent the plot.

mp.scatter(X,Y)

mp.show()

To ensure the chart is more readable, write down the X and Y axes. This can be achieved using the xlabel and ylabel forms of pyplot.

mp.scatter(X,Y)

mp.xlabel('Production revenue in USD')

mp.ylabel('Worldwide gross in USD')

mp.show()

Train the Algorithm

You can now run the regression on the plot to evaluate the results. Here, the key goal is to create a straight line or a line of expected values that will serve as a guide to any possible forecasts. As you may have noticed, there are many modules that have specific features. You must use Scikit-learn, which is a very common machine learning application, to run the regression. Back in the import loop, add a new line to load linear regression from the Scikit-learn module and re-run.

import pandas as pd

from pandas import DataFrame as df

import matplotlib.pyplot as mp

from sklearn.linear_model import LinearRegression

```
In [*]:  import pandas as pd
         from pandas import DataFrame as df
         import matplotlib.pyplot as mp
         from sklearn.linear_model import LinearRegression
```

Scikit-learn allows you to construct a linear regression model. Since the task of running a linear regression is performed by an entity, you would need to construct a new entity, in this case the regression object name. The Fit approach can be used to adapt the regression model to the results. In other words, you have to know the pattern using the training details. Using the suit form as seen below for this reason.

regressionObject = LinearRegression();

regressionObject.fit(X,Y)

```
In [10]:  regressionObject = LinearRegression();

In [11]:  regressionObject.fit(X,Y)
Out[11]:  LinearRegression(copy_X=True, fit_intercept=True, n_jobs=None,
                normalize=False)
```

When the model has been conditioned with the training dataset, you can predict the value of Y using the regression variable. The predictive approach will help you determine Y values for each X.

Then yPredicted is equivalent to regressionObject.predict(X), and then yPredicted is used to construct the regression line to the plot using this argument. You will find that I used the green color for the regression line, which is seen successfully in the map. Edit the previous cell to include the plot.

mp.scatter(X,Y)

```
mp.xlabel('Production revenue in USD')

mp.ylabel('Worldwide gross in USD')

mp.plot(X, regressionObject.predict(X), color = 'green')

mp.show
```

Analyze

As you can see from the storyline, there's a good relationship between the two principles. When manufacturing sales rise, there is an increase in total profits worldwide. This assumes that the shift rate of vector Y is equal to the increase in X. In case the regression line is linear, the line equation is Y = aX + b, the a is the regression coefficient/slope of the line, which implies the variance of Y with the increase in the values of X.

The positive regression coefficient (a) tells you that the relationship between X and Y is positive. The coefficient value can be calculated using the coef property of the regression variable. For this figure, the correlation coefficient is 3.11, which means that you will get $3.11 in exchange for each USD spent on film production.

```
regressionObject.coef_
```

```
In [9]:  regressionObject.coef_
Out[9]:  array([[3.11150918]])
```

The next stage is to determine b the line intercept_. It can be achieved using the intercept property on the regression variable.

regressionObject.intercept_

```
In [11]:  regressionObject.intercept_
Out[11]:  array([-7236192.72913958])
```

The generalized line formula is Y = aX + b. Now imagine a hypothetical situation where you want to estimate the world's income for a movie made for $20 million in the production budget. The calculation can be calculated by substituting the values in the equation.

Y = 3.11150918 * 20,000,000 + (-7236192.72913958)

Y = 54,993,990.87086042

The following calculation can be extracted using the Python notebook as follows:

Create the pandas DataFrame with our movie Budget

data = [[20000000]]

dfBudget = df(data, columns = ['Estimated_Budget'])

dfBudget

regressionObject.coef_[0][0] * dfBudget.loc[0]['Estimated_Budget'] + regressionObject.intercept_[0]

```
In [21]: # Create the pandas DataFrame with our movie Budget
         data = [[20000000]]
         dfBudget = df(data, columns = ['Estimated_Budget'])
         dfBudget

Out[21]:
            Estimated_Budget
         0     20000000

In [20]: regressionObject.coef_[0][0] * dfBudget.loc[0]['Estimated_Budget'] + regressionObject.intercept_[0]
Out[20]: 54993990.929582946
```

The main thing to remember here is that the model is a conceptual interpretation of the data presented. The predictions are not 100% correct, but there is a strong probability that the predictions could turn out to be valid. Bear in mind that this paradigm is a radical simplification of the real world.

HOW TO APPLY AI TO
YOUR MARKETING

Artificial Intelligence (AI) is a significant driver to smooth consumer service and helps advertisers predict what their clients want. Working on this statistical technology, digital marketing is certainly one of the most successful ways to target an audience.

The short facts on AI Artificial Intelligence are the technology that allows robots to solve challenges in the same way that humans do. Computer programs have been programmed manually for decades in order to deliver a particular output from a particular entry. When using AI, machines can use data to identify patterns and make decisions without being specifically trained to do so.

One-to-one optimization by AI.

There is a growing emphasis on customized messaging in marketing today. Marketing campaigns ROI can be dramatically enhanced with the use of sophisticated analytics, CRM as well as social media. Together, these three technologies allow a strategic, multi-layer strategy that defines, recognizes and automatically produces personalized communications.

Focusing on one-to-one optimization rather than one-to-million is more about knowing the customers: what they need, what they desire, and what they think of. By knowing this, you should be able to have the right answer and the right message for each person. Once you enter a genuine one-to-one marketing approach, AI may be used to reduce the number of encounters that consumers have with the company, so that it is only certain encounters of real meaning that they associate of.

This has to be handled automatically, and the AI-based tools are there to help. Solutions automate in real-time, with personalized notifications for each client who always gets the correct prompts in order to help them enter the next level of their buying process, resulting in more purchases and more ROI.

AI lets advertisers evolve more. Due to improved modelling algorithms using machine learning, new innovations can be regularly evaluated more. An organization that leverages artificial learning to test-is capable of helping companies out-innovate their rivals.

Human and computer communication with the best outcomes.

Accelerated developments have now taken technologies such as AI to the level that it can actually contend with the efficiency and accuracy of a human being. Yeah, how are you going to get the best results for this new technology? As stated in the book "The Second Machine Age" by Erik Brynjolfsson and Andrew McAfee, a machine-aided human player, could be able to defeat a robot. This means that mixing professional communications with state-of-the-art technologies is a winning recipe.

You're going to need experts to make sense of the data and find out how to turn new ideas from more advanced AI into new tactics. The capabilities of AI-based software are a good start, but the true game-changer would be how advertisers want to use the information they have gained in new directions that are yet to be explored. This is where we get to see the real importance of AI in marketing. Well, outside artificial intelligence, human intelligence will definitely continue to play a major role in the use of AI.

AI applied to marketing.

Some of the things that AI can do when it comes to marketing are mentioned below:

Optimization of ads

AI-based marketing software helps you to conduct A / B marketing testing in a way that saves time as well as resources and enables the development of quality advertising content with as little time as possible by using machine learning algorithms. The computer automatically partitions budgets across channels to optimize ROI. Optimizes thousands of micro-campaigns per minute and builds on new approaches. Using the support of automation, you can still maintain consumer experience knowledge for potential marketing and use the most cost-effective touchpoints in order to generate ROI.

Training Conduct constant

A-B monitoring across thousands of factors, including innovative ones. AI is growing its performance faster than human. This is partly due to the fact that AI can make use of minute bits of knowledge to try to make a guess.

Automated and tailored content.

With AI-based technologies, multimedia creatives can be designed to be configured for one-to-one communication instead of mass communication. This is achieved dynamically within a fraction of a second and on a wide scale, thus allowing advertisers to send a customized message to the customer. This has proved to be a perfect way to increase the ROI of a marketing campaign.

Semantic research

AI-based techniques are used to define, and process language constructs in classes and documents on the basis of the requirements used to identify word patterns.

Chatbot Creation

The Chatbot is defined as an artificial intelligence platform that handles clients at an individual level. This is a cost-effective approach that tackles less complicated consumer problems. The New York Times, for example, sends nearly 300 messages a day on its social media networks. Back in the days, a person had to post each of these messages manually, but instead, the newspaper developed a chatbot in order to manage social posts automatically. Today, it also forecasts which stories are doing well and which ones need to be more promoted. With the bot automating the task, the human developer gets more time to commit to the innovative aspect the AI just can't manage.

Intelligent decisions

Analytics applications such as Google Analytics 360 Suite and Adobe Analytics are based on AI technologies that offer a robust platform for data-driven decisions. Through reviewing past data, both physical touchpoints and competitor data, computers will tell us exactly what works and what doesn't work. Machines are able to interrupt specifics and provide insightful input about potential next moves.

Getting the right user, at the right time, in the right place.

AI encourages digital ads by segmenting the best audiences on the basis of demographics such as occupation, employment, salary, desires, gender as well as age. For digital ads, prospective buyers will easily sit at home and search websites on their smartphones and desktops for the most wanted object. AI-based applications make sure you meet the right user, at the right time and in the right place.

Increased marketing income

With AI Used in a wise manner, AI will transform the marketing investment into more sales and improved branding experience.

John Wanamaker, a successful US communications visionary, invented the term, "Half the money I spend on ads is wasted; the trouble is, I don't know which half." Luckily, it's no longer true for us. By combining smart machines and smart men, we will be able to ensure that any project, big or small, does what it needs to do: maximize the income of our clients.

HOW TO APPLY AI TO
SOCIAL MEDIA

A successful social media campaign is important to the marketing plan of any company. Yet getting one is better said than done. In reality, only 48% of businesses report that they receive a favorable ROI from their social media.

While there are many explanations for this, it is safe to say that social media marketing is not as simple as it used to be. Facebook and Instagram's algorithm update have almost destroyed organic traffic. In fact, businesses will need to spend a significant amount of time working on content creation, tailored Facebook advertising (not to be confused with pay-per-click or PPC marketing), influencer marketing, customer support, and keep up to date with current social developments.

It's no surprise digital marketers are willing to incorporate AI into their social media campaign.

Luckily, the future is here for all of us. AI and machine learning technologies are in full swing; thus, they're not going anywhere fast. Learning how to use this innovative tool will streamline your workflow as well as create a stronger user experience for those who connect with your media feeds.

Here are three ways in which you can integrate artificial intelligence into your social media strategy:

Interact with your followers using chatbots.

While chatbots are still in their development, they are already in use by marketers to simplify communications with their customers. In reality, according to Entrepreneur, there are more than 1.3 billion users on Facebook Messenger. Yet there are just 300,000 bots on the Messenger site. With such a large user base and low pricing, there are endless opportunities to connect and communicate with your clients too.

One of the most critical features of Chatbots is that they are entirely adjustable. They're doing a variety of roles. Chatbots may initiate a dialogue with a potential customer by engaging with one of your social posts or ads.

Bots may also support your customers with AI and machine learning by responding to questions they might have about a certain product or service. Some bots also have the potential to connect your customers from a Facebook network to a product listed on your website.

Chatbots can be used to check up on previous clients as well. You can give them coupons, discounts and exclusive sales through automatic social media messages.

AI bots are also great examples of customer service. We will provide customer service 24/7 with no overhead.

Perhaps, one of the biggest advantages of using a Chatbot is the immense feedback you receive from your clients. You will be able to monitor and evaluate consumer data to re-target clients, boost user experience, and eventually maximize sales.

Increase your strategic intelligence.

AI-based programs now enable marketers to perform in-depth competition analysis. Instead of combing your competitor's Facebook posts manually in order to see what kind of content is doing well, artificial intelligence algorithms will do the heavy lifting for you.

Getting AI to do a strategic analysis gives you a massive benefit as well. For one thing, it saves you a lot of time and energy. Perhaps, most importantly, it gives you the evidence you couldn't find by looking at the state of Facebook. AI will predict how many experiences have accrued and how many to hit every particular post. This perspective will help you make data-driven choices about the kind of content the company wants to produce.

It's still hard enough to contend on social media. Why don't you find it easy to have AI on your side?

Optimize your promotion efforts.

Most digital marketers may likely agree with the following comment, "If you create it, it won't come." The development of effective social media content needs research, preparation, implementation as well as promotion. Overall, advertising is one of the 4Ps in the marketing mix.

So, how is AI able to assist with the promotion? AI gives you data to help advertisers make smarter, data-driven decisions. As mentioned above, you can understand what kind of posts and advertisements are doing well. Machine learning predicts what kind of content best performs on the basis of quality, timing, competition as well as audience. Using AI, advertisers will decide whether to make the best of their advertising budgets.

How to apply AI to Customer behavior and Product Pricing.

The conversation about AI in retail is constant, but it's no longer just talking: AI is here. Its impact, though recent, is evident and it is rapidly evolving retail. According to WBR Insights, over half (57%) of retailers plan to invest in AI over the next five years to address logistics challenges and boost customer service.

Clearly, if the rivals don't even use AI, they'll be in the near future. Companies can no longer rely on seasonal and historical data to be effective. This new approach is tailored to the accuracy and precision that only AI and machine learning have. Such emerging innovations, combined with the Internet of Things (IoT) and analytical info, are generating better consumer service and increasing the competitive bar. Nevertheless, whenever it gets to the retail arena, nothing is more critical than quality, and retailers who are willing to use AI to gain an edge in this region will have a massive advantage.

Where AI is able to send you the advantage

Previously, we saw retailers focusing on guesswork, playing a massive game called 'The Price is Right.' However, the strategy has to be more pragmatic in today's hyper-competitive environment. Pricing is a tool that helps retailers to create high-performance, competitive demand which should be aligned with retailers' approach to variety management, merchandising and localization. It will also help the brand and the manner in which it is advertised and placed. Retailers tend to find the right price in the right place and at the right time.

Price optimization was used to mean a conventional statistical analysis of how consumers participate in various product and service pricing across each channel; thus, the organization could measure rates that comply with market goals and optimize profits.

Nowadays, it's all about data: efficient price optimization will extend forecasting in a range of machine learning as well as optimization sciences. Machine learning sets processes for rational product categories (assortments and product lines) through periods (seasons, weeks and months) and positions (price zones, online and in-store touchpoints). Then, by AI, market optimization will begin to forecast, switching from a reactive to a proactive model.

Look ahead rather than backward

Retailers used to focus on historical demand to drive prices, continuously attempting to find out what will happen in the future on the basis of what happens in the past. All of that has improved today, as AI will add in hundreds of other more up-to-date factors, ranging from market habits and consumer signatures to contextual details such as temperature, current affairs and public holidays.

AI and machine learning have the opportunity to drill down on these cases, offering greater perspectives than ever before. This could help retailers, for example, to evaluate trend communication through social media and measure a more accurate likelihood of demand rates. Through these tools, retailers can create actionable data to manage customer tastes and demand and deliver more customized shopping experiences than ever before. The most sophisticated AI technologies don't just make forecasts and recommendations; they are able to boost the demand efficiency with reliable real-time data that generates more sales and profitability.

More pricing, more cash

AI and machine learning technologies allow retailers to use competitive pricing models that prevent surplus supply, with fewer items not sold around the business. Retailers will either change their price plan at the end of the season or where any surplus product has to be packaged.

AI will help dramatically to minimize waste as well. It achieves so by forecasting consumer demand and making accurate price choices for all markets. Instead, thanks to its knowledge of the complex relationship between price volatility and demand, AI will ensure that the stock goes where it is most required.

The price is right.

As companies are able to access shopper data and broader perspectives from AI and machine learning, they are more likely to behave creatively, concentrating more on their consumer experience around the board. Given a lot of concern about AI in the retail industry and what it means for jobs. The reality is that technology such as machine learning and AI help more retailers to make their stores competitive and their staff concentrate on programs that will certainly increase consumer engagement. Most notably, AI and machine learning are making guesswork out of pricing.

4 Ways AI can help elevate your online marketing systems

Artificial Intelligence (AI) adoption in marketing is at the forefront of exciting opportunities, and we are currently experiencing an AI "gold rush." The effect of AI and machine learning (ML) is amazing, and as business owners and digital marketers, you will surely reap stunning benefits.

Marketing AI is promising — making approaches more effective, clever and consumer-friendly.

As a leading small business company, it's just natural that you, too, would like to purchase gold and get that strategic edge from the state-of-the-art AI enterprise marketing software and eventually more profits.

So, the question is not whether to engage in AI, but how to consistently analyze the problem situations in your business in order to accelerate AI-powered approaches and then move forward at lightning speed.

AI is far beyond the short-term win point. With well-established, tried-and-tested marketing strategies and creative applications, you are able to boost your brand image and enhance the customer experience.

Over the next decade, you should predict a dramatic change as AI-powered marketing tools drive innovation to connect and improve your potential users.

We'll highlight four common AI Ways that can help elevate your online marketing systems. If the cause is obvious, then how it will automatically fall! Does that sound like a confusing philosophy?

Essentially, it's pretty simple — when you're persuaded about the AI advantages (why), you'll definitely find opportunities to use AI in the marketing field.

Now let us begin by looking at some ways to boost the marketing efforts by using AI.

1. Forecasting Customer Behavior with propensity Models.

Data is at the center of decision making. Online data can be enhanced with computational power and probabilistic prediction models. Algorithms will cycle through data to make more accurate business decisions in real-time.

How fascinating would it be if you know about the opportunities that are most likely to react to the offer?

With predictive scorecards such as Likelihood models, the recognition of future customers became a fact.

Machine Learning has opened the power of propensity modelling — and improved with propensity scores — you can consider the probability of a particular consumer transacting and calculating the importance of the consumer.

As AdWords experts, you can gain feedback and suggested approaches to meet the ideal marketing goals — all you need to do is use AI to identify the target demographic to campaign objectives. Your inputs will act as a catalyst for an automated strategy guidance method.

The methodology is very formal, and all you need to do is define goals for data extraction, create and test models as well as monitor the tests.

You should start by looking at the company and list the problem case scenarios. Reflection exercise should promote the analysis of your company goals and available data sources in order to identify trends that match your needs.

Data extraction should be possible at this stage. Next, before choosing the final pattern, you will use data mining. You should test the models based on the goals you have previously set.

Finally, you will adopt the findings of the model to business decisions and achieve better outcomes. You will find it beneficial to constantly tweak the templates that will promote best-in-class outcomes.

2. Load Time Reduction Using Accelerated Mobile Page (AMP).

Imagine the post being included in the News Carousel — that would be amazing, wouldn't it?

Through AI influencing SEO, you will find that the digital marketing sphere has been changed. You can use the Accelerated Mobile Page (AMP) in order to reduce load time and find the content in key location areas.

With an AMP listing, you can also increase the chances of your blog appearing in Google's top three search results and attract more organic web traffic.

If you want to promote content consumption and your platform is already mobile-friendly, AMP may be the right choice for you.

Some of the big brand names use AMPs — eBay produced AMP versions of their product listing pages, and it was a proof of concept that shop sites could use AMPs for mid-funnel content.

3. Creating Personalized Experiences using Intelligent Algorithms.

Talk about it — if you get marketing emails that are specifically geared to your needs, what happens? You've heard it! You are more likely to engage in text communications. You will make most of the advantages you already have with AI marketing tools.

The future of marketing will, therefore, be influenced by the integration of activities and the development of customized content that will promote unique experiences for each consumer.

The Uberflip cloud-based content platform makes it easy to tailor marketing and scale B2B marketers with a diverse audience. The app produces revenue-generating opportunities and not only increases interaction, attracts leads, but can also optimize content in order to achieve your particular goals.

Aizimov is another fascinating AI program that operates on custom and tailored messages on your behalf.

The app browses the internet for social media, news and financial documents and creates relevant emails and messages for each of the target audiences.

How is the tool working?

The software is designed to evaluate the psychological profile of the individual and then agree on the type of message to be generated and how to write it. It also chooses the best medium, such as Facebook, Instagram, LinkedIn, and more, in order to reach out to every prospect.

AI will improve the user experience with smart automation on your web. Through analyzing data points, AI can view customized content and evaluate users 'positions, apps, profiles, previous experiences, and more. Insights help to simplify email campaigns and to submit daily push alerts to prospects focused on micro-moments.

You can consider clever algorithms that configure push alerts. With push alerts driven by behavioral automation, you can send unique messages to particular users and deliver the appropriate message at the right time.

Take Pandora, for instance — it recommends new songs that listeners would enjoy based on machine learning algorithms. Music listening apps are achieving a strategic advantage in order to bring the best user experience.

Algorithms also boost website experiences — AI will view best-fitting deals and content by evaluating hundreds of data points for a single user.

Personalization can help to create compelling user experiences — although app optimization remains one of the biggest challenges for marketers, with constant algorithm refinement, you will find a crazy amount of things that can be done by using AI software.

4. AI-Powered Data Creation.

You need to build it before you can customize content. With AI software, content creation will add real value to marketers producing high-performance content across every touchpoint and channel.

Automated production of business-related content is still on demand. According to Gartner, by 2018, 20% of all market content was projected to be generated by machines.

Even though there has been no significant increase in the automated production of business-related content as expected, the prediction remains viable, and the global research company anticipates more automated creation of business content.

Digital content production can be found in business content, including:

- Contracts and reports.
- Summaries of income and expense.
- Real-time market insight.
- Guided post.
- Financial accounts, press releases and news stories.
- Customized correspondence, and more.

You will find a plethora of AI tools that can promote content development with ease and simplicity.

Acrolinx is a phenomenal forum that allows businesses to strategically coordinate content production.

The platform lets you create highly efficient content on a scale.

The app reads your content and uses the AI engine to analyze your content, score it, and then help you create improved content. Global brands like IBM, Google, and Facebook are using Acrolinx to deliver enterprise-wide on-target content.

You can get suggestions for fresh social media content that your brand's fans are likely to engage with Rocco's AI-powered marketing tool.

Interactive advertising is another factor that is essential to social media marketing strategies. With Stackla, it is possible to discover user-generated content (UGC) and convert it into meaningful content that connects users.

Using geolocation, keywords, hashtags, and sophisticated visual recognition technologies, Stackla finds the best graphics from any social network and puts together all images in order to create actionable user interactions at every touchpoint of the customer.

You should test out the latest AI applications and determine how they suit the business needs, and then create meaningful content using AI and ML.

3 Ways to Automate boring tasks with AI

Ensure more efficient business compliance methods with AI

Today, two main innovations transforming the Compliance industry are artificial intelligence (AI) and machine learning. Contrarily to popular opinion, these new technologies are not expected to replace human workers. In reality, they are engineered to make human work simpler and more fun. For instance, robotic process automation (RPA) can execute routine, time-consuming processes tirelessly and more effectively than humans can, allowing employees to concentrate on facets of their jobs that involve emotional intelligence, logic as well as human interaction. The well-suited RPA activities include filling out paperwork, data processing, and copying and pasting documents through formats and agencies.

Artificial intelligence can be extended to more complex activities that can perform more useful business purposes. Although RPA includes structured data in a spreadsheet or archive, AI might make sense of unstructured data such as e-mails, phone calls, documents, and contracts. Most specifically, AI can conduct complex analysis, such as identifying patterns, optimizing pathways, understanding expression and inflection, and personalizing information. As a result, AI has the ability to minimize costs and improve the productivity of third-party risk control, thus allowing workers the opportunity to do their duties more efficiently.

So, what does that mean for you and your business? Potential advantages are easy to see, but many businesses have failed to effectively adopt the technology, partly because of financial commitment and partly because of a lack of awareness of how and where to proceed. If Robots Respond to Compliance, businesses that have been successful have begun a low-cost project in order to determine the value of the product before making a larger investment. E.g., most businesses have readily accessible data on accounts payable. AI can instead be used to recognize outliers, anomalies, and trends, such as high spending by a single employee or in a particular area. This could help to simplify the risk management process, which would also be supervised by human data analysts but made more effective by AI.

The potential benefits of these emerging technologies to compliance practitioners are just extraordinary. For example, the AI-driven framework will anticipate problems before they really become problems. Such a program is capable of tracking the entire life cycle of an account with the potential to collect more than 1,000 primary risk indicators (KRIs) per account. In the case of a transaction exceeding the appropriate risk threshold as defined by the program, the enforcement department is obligated to review, thus the false negatives and concentrating resources on real problems. Thanks to machine learning, the amount of KRIs a program can catch is increasingly growing, and the risk tolerance paradigm is then being established.

Nevertheless, the most critical aspect of the performance of such a device is the human touch. To order to transform the system's findings into practical resources, qualified Compliance practitioners are required to understand the data and to take action. And when complemented by AI, enforcement officers are able to make crucial choices using real-time observations. The benefits of incorporating this form of information in the enforcement department will extend well across the business, from marketing and customer support, which turns into better customer interaction.

The Future of Compliance.

What are the consequences for practitioners of these technologies? The immense changes they are making, especially in the financial and accounting fields, definitely have the potential to improve Compliance by increasing productivity and thus facilitating greater coordination between departments and other agencies. Moreover, the Compliance environment itself is still changing rapidly, allowing space for divergence between regulatory authorities and companies implementing emerging technology, eventually increasing obstacles to adoption. As technical and regulatory environments continue to grow, it will be important for leaders to remain on top of developments in all fields in order to allow their companies to minimize costs and improve productivity while still fulfilling their commitments in order to protect the privacy of consumers and to satisfy compliance criteria.

HOW ARTIFICIAL INTELLIGENCE WILL CHANGE THE NATURE OF BUSINESS IN THE FUTURE

―――――――――○―――――――――

Technology is evolving over time and is moving rapidly towards a workplace where people work together with machines. Artificial intelligence (AI) and machine learning algorithms are transforming our way of manufacturing products and performing customer service. AI is improving human experiences, especially when it comes to speech recognition and voice detection.

From virtual chatbots to electronic orders, AI plays a crucial function on a daily basis. While these technical developments are ongoing, new forms of market opportunities are emerging, leading to high productivity. AI technologies in the industry predict economic development that is impactful due to big developments in human activity. AI is becoming more popular at a phenomenal rate and will have a major impact on how we work out our routine.

AI teaming up with humans.

AI is the basis of a range of innovative inventions in today's world. The AI-enabled approach reduces the difference between human and machine experiences. AI was created to understand the human being and his relationship with technology. This is also helping us push into a world where we are interdependent.

AI links the relationship between humans and computers more tightly. Human data teaches intelligent technologies and computers that help AI mimic aspects of human intelligence. Thinking about AI, the more it thinks about the human experience, the smarter it improves.

Smart Processing.

Nowadays, robotics is seeking to replace humans with bots because it connects as humanely as possible. It can also be seen that the robots of these days are now responsible for a substantial part of the daily work of several industries. From robotic handling to answering customer support requests, computer execution is getting smarter and more efficient thanks to AI integration.

As a part of this development, more businesses are opting to incorporate AI in their market system. In this situation, the extent of deployment would ensure that workers are happy with AI. While AI lets workers understand the process better by allowing robots to increase human capabilities.

Cutting-edge Analysis.

AI is the best way to evaluate patterns of use and then utilize machine learning to find insights into a particular process. AI also affects companies with an innovative technology audit, allowing workers to boost overall customer service.

We are living in an age where small and large technology-related issues are happening at a quite fast rate. AI is known as a genuinely transformative tool because it helps companies to do a more insight-driven analysis. Businesses are creating sophisticated AI-enabled applications for machine learning and real-time application automation that affect how consumers function.

Learning new skills.

AI is driving computers that are able to interact with humans in speech, allowing them to understand more and more. As a consequence, when it comes to mastering new technology-related skills, the AI-based machine mastering workforce becomes more agile.

Employees as an employee will reap the advantages of AI as the business expands with the introduction of AI. This allows companies to raise sales with reduced costs and boost overall customer loyalty. Businesses also need to build a workplace where workers can learn more and thus grow more.

Bottom line.

AI is now changing the way we communicate on a regular basis. For sophisticated embedded technologies such as cloud systems, AI can be used to find a new information and produce insights quickly. AI also has the ability to enhance workplace engagement by improving decision-making.

The future is full of solution-enabled AI applications or strategies that can be used to forecast consumer behavior. It would allow any size of the company to connect, interpret information at the right time across the right digital network.

12 OF THE MOST POPULAR ARTIFICIAL INTELLIGENCE TOOLS IN THE MARKET

A rtificial intelligence currently pervades many aspects of our lives and is here to remain in the near future. This bird's eye view of the best open-source AI applications serves as a reminder of how AI has already shaped our lives.

Imagine the simulated world in which you're eating in a restaurant. In this hypothetical example, from the food served on your plate to the waiter who takes care of you, everything has been planned according to your taste as well as temperament, without asking you a single question.

Picture a world in which only the angle at which the meal is prepared in this restaurant or the grin of the waiter can be measured with possible recommendations in order to match your style or mood. In such a given scenario, if you're trying to buy a pair of shoes, you'd make a few swipes on your mobile, and all the shoes available in your favorite color, with the exact shape of the sole and the height of the heel, would appear on your computer. This is all due to machine learning (ML)—and the possibilities are definitely infinite.

Artificial intelligence or AI has infiltrated several aspects of our lives. Let's just think about 2018! Many of these speech recognition technologies that we use to search and power our smartphones are the beginning of a new age. We have not grasped the full range of AI yet. A small edition of AI technology is now installed inside our vehicles. Apple's Siri, Google's OK Google, and Amazon's Alexa apps are also in operation, thus monitoring your sound and speech along with addressing your question. These AI-backed platforms provide a natural language processing network and are capable of responding to commands. You will now get directions to the venue and search for a similar restaurant, all of this by simply rubbing your fingers on the phone!

Currently, driverless vehicles are being developed, and the population of robots is on the rise, as they are predicted to replace humans in certain areas in the very distant future. You might imagine robot hotel receptionists and robots to clean our houses, transforming us to couch potatoes. Yeah, well, let's stick to the lighter side of the matter!

Machine learning is a part of artificial intelligence that works closely with computer self-learning. This ensures that machines learn to evolve and adapt easily without the need for programming.

And automation is defined as a new digital technology that no longer needs human help in any process. In other words, this is considered as a programed function. This method uses various management mechanisms for specific processes or devices, such as automated machinery, assembly lines, boilers, telecommunications networks, containers, aircraft and vehicles, meaning that there is little or less human intervention. A few processes have even been fully computerized.

The automation that we know today started with basic devices, which include water wheels, in the 11th century. Gradually, people have started to build these basic devices and to evolve over time.

Now let's look at 12 of the Market's Most Common Artificial Intelligence tools.

Apache Mahout: This is an open-source machine learning platform under the Apache License. It was originally designed to improve work on common math problems involving statistics and linear algebra. This ML tool was developed by the Apache Software Foundation and is based on a framework called Mahout Hadoop. Data researchers use this open-source deep learning platform in order to conduct a crucial and thorough study of Big

Data. Comprehension of objective data allows to derive valuable information and to recognize patterns. Mahout algorithms help users cluster and group Big Data by first saving data to the Hadoop Distributed File System. It has a cross-operating system and offers users an R- syntax environment.

Link: https:/mahut.apache.org/.

Distributed Machine Learning Toolkit (DMTK): it's just an opensource ML tool that simplifies various Big Data activities. DMTK was launched by Microsoft, with new and sophisticated algorithms being added to this toolkit on a regular basis. This toolkit helps researchers to work with algorithms by changing and tweaking them according to their needs. Historically, researchers needed a lot of computing capital to work on Big Data, since it has been proven that larger data models contribute to improved performance, but that became very difficult. DMTK allows creativity in both system algorithms and ML algorithms.

Link: http:/www.dmtk.io/.

Open Neural Networks (OpenNN): is an opensource library coded in the C++ language. It has been built for in- learning and for the application of neural networks. This library has an easy--, deep architecture and is used in advanced ML study. This opensource library is being used in vertical logistics and marketing.

OpenNN allows high- computing as well, as it has a faster processor speed.

Link: http:/www.openn.net/.

OpenCyc: It is an opensource knowledge resource that makes text comprehension possible. Cycorp released OpenCyc to guarantee that consumers have free access to this knowledge base so that they can use OpenCyc in numerous applications. OpenCyc's extensive knowledgebase contains a wide variety of definitions, data, taxonomies, statements and laws. It is accessible in two ways, i.e. ontology and semantic web endpoints. The above can also be referred to as permanent URIs, which means that all RDF versions and human- types are returned to users.

Cycorp allows users to browse through a vast archive and analyze the related information in order to provide correct analysis. This helps differentiate the relative terms and synonyms of a single key search term and assures that the app operates just like an individual, thus demonstrating human cognitive ability and discernment. OpenCyc has supported AI developers with their initiatives and that they can now use their ontologies to ensure machine learning (ML) that can be disrupted by humans to deter machines from doing damage. Cyc has revolutionized ML by allowing applications to understand the deep theory and reasoning of the human mind.

Link: http:/www.cyc.com / opendec/.

H2O: This open-source ML development platform, developed by H2O.ai, is used by programmers and AI researchers. It is written in R, Python and Java programming languages and is used for predictive data processing by AI researchers as well as developers on any software platform they are familiar with. It can also be used to evaluate data sets in the cloud and Apache Hadoop file systems. It supports various operating systems — Linux, MacOS, and Microsoft Windows.

This open-source deep learning framework aims to make predictions through an in- of the data. This way the user can derive valuable lessons. Having two open source versions, this platform has been extensively used for statistical modelling, health care and fraud detection too.

Link: https:/www.h2o.ai/.

TensorFlow: Such an open-source ML library has been introduced by Google Brain. It helps you to write libraries for dataflow programming. This functions in two programming languages — C++ and Python. TensorFlow has been developed by Google for better AI applications. This was originally introduced for use in Gmail, Google Images and Google Search. This open-source AI platform is also used by programmers for numerical computing. TensorFlow's easy-- interface and architecture helps you to access the different frameworks. There is no limit on its usability. You will use it for TPUs, CPUs and GPUs. You can have it on your Mac as well, cell phone or tablet. This method is useful in supporting researchers with their computational calculation and neural network applications. TensorFlow was released under the Apache 2.0 Open Source License in 2015.

Link: https:/www.tensorflow.org.

Deeplearning4j: As its name suggests, Deeplearning4j is an open-source Java AI platform specially designed for deep learning. It was published under the Apache License 2.0, produced by a group of AI researchers which is situated in San Francisco and Tokyo.

It uses its own deep learning library built for Java Virtual Machine (JVM). This library is called ND4J, which deals on both CPUs which GPUS. The architecture is used for the creation of neural networks and has several sophisticated visualization methods. This method has a wide variety of scientific uses and is used in the fields of information security as well as image recognition. It has been combined with other open-source AI projects such as Keta and TensorFlow. This can be found in a variety of API languages such as Python and Clojure.

Link: https:/deeplearning4j.org.

Caffe: This is an open-source AI platform developed by the Berkeley Vision and Learning Center. It supports deep learning and is capable of storing millions of images per day. It has a phenomenal pace and was published under the BSD 2-Clause license. This complex AI method has been translated to C++ and has a Python GUI. It comes with an amazing architecture that lets you switch between the CPU and the GPU. This AI method is being used by scientific researchers in several projects and has also established large- implementations in the area of multimedia and vision.

Link: http:/caffe.berkeleyvision.org/.

ONNX (Open Neural Network Exchange): ONNX serves as an opensource AI format which is commonly used by AI researchers in deep learning models. It's mainly a Facebook open-source initiative; however, it's still funded by Microsoft and AWS. This open-source deep learning platform was established in 2017 when both tech companies, Facebook and Microsoft, came together in order to build an ML application switching program.

Microsoft has contributed to the project by incorporating the Cognitive Toolkit and Brainwave Project Platform. This interface allows users to add their creative materials, such as extensible computer graphics templates and it also allows them to change their networks according to their specifications.

Link: https:/onnx.ai/.

Oryx 2: It is an opensource application based on Spark and Apache Kafka. Oryx 2 supports real- learning on a wider scale. This framework is being used by AI researchers for the development of applications as well as for grouping and clustering.

Link: http:/orix.io/.

Apache SystemML: This is a scalable open-source AI framework that focuses on Big Data and has been designed in order to address complex mathematical issues. This could be applied to both Spark and Hadoop. It's working on a Python- R syntax. It is applied to deep learning with GPUs and to neural network architectures for processing.

Link: https:/systemml.apache.org.

MLlib: It was introduced by Apache Spark and it is a machine learning platform utilized for learning algorithms. This AI framework uses a number of commonly used programming languages such as R, Scala, Java and Python. It will run on a number of platforms, including Hadoop, Kubernetes or in the cloud. This library includes a number of deep learning and key ML algorithms. It makes ML simpler and more realistic for AI researchers.

10 AI Trends for Businesses

Most people often equate artificial intelligence with science fiction dystopias, but the image is waning as artificial intelligence grows and becomes more prevalent in our daily lives. Nowadays, artificial intelligence is a household name (and occasionally even a household appearance – hello, Alexa!).

While the adoption of artificial intelligence in modern culture is a recent development, it is definitely not a new idea. The scientific field of artificial intelligence came into being in 1956, but it took decades of research to make substantial strides in creating an artificial intelligence program and transforming it a technical reality.

Artificial intelligence has a wide variety of applications in industry. In reality, most of us engage with artificial intelligence in one way or another on a daily basis. From the ordinary to the spectacular, artificial intelligence is challenging nearly any market activity in every industry. When artificial intelligence innovations proliferate, it is becoming crucial for companies who wish to keep a competitive advantage.

A lot of work has been going on within the field of artificial intelligence. We cannot draw a map of how AI is advancing. Nonetheless, we should look around for technology that draws a lot of interest and is trending for business;

1. AI will gradually track as well as optimize business processes.

While the first robots in the workforce were mainly involved in automating manual tasks such as packaging and production lines, today's software-based robots are able to do the routine yet necessary work that we normally do on computers. Filling in documents, creating reports and graphs, and providing paperwork and instructions are all things that can be done by computers that track what we do and learn to do for us in a simpler and more efficient manner. Such technology – known as robotic process technology – would release us from time- yet necessary manual duties, therefore enabling us to focus more time on dynamic, political, innovative, and interpersonal activities.

2. Constant personalization will take place in real-time.

This phenomenon is powered by the rise of Web companies like Amazon, Alibaba, and Google, and their ability to offer customized content as well as advice. AI helps products and services suppliers to easily and reliably visualize a 360-degree vision of consumers in real- as they connect through web platforms and smartphone devices, thus rapidly discovering how their forecasts will match our expectations and desires with ever- precision. Much as food delivery services like Dominos will know where we are most likely to order food and make sure that the "Buy Now" icon is in front of us at the right time, every other company will

certainly build strategies aimed at providing personalized consumer service on a scale.

3. AI is becoming more valuable as data becomes more reliable
and accessible.

The accuracy of the knowledge available is also an obstacle to
businesses and organizations wanting to move into automated
AI-driven decision-making. Nevertheless, as techniques and approaches for simulating real- processes and structures in the digital realm have advanced in recent years, reliable data has become
increasingly available. Simulations have progressed to the point
where carmakers and those working on the production of self-
cars can receive thousands of hours of driving data without ever
leaving the facility, leading to significant cost savings and an improvement in the accuracy of the data that might be obtained.
Why incur the cost and danger of checking AI systems in the real
world when computers are now efficient enough and educated on
precise enough data to replicate anything in the digital world?
2020 will see an improvement in the precision and affordability
of real- models, which, in effect, will lead to more efficient and
reliable AIs.

4. More computers are using AI-powered technology.

As the equipment and skills required to implement AI are cheaper and more available, we will continue to see it used in a growing number of tools, gadgets, and applications. In 2019, we're already used to run applications that send us AI-powered forecasts on our machines, tablets, and watches as well. As the next decade passes and the cost of hardware and software begin to fall, AI technologies will gradually be integrated into our cars, home appliances, and office devices. Advanced technologies such as virtual and augmented reality interfaces and paradigms such as the cloud and the Internet of Things, the next year, will see more and more machines of several shapes and sizes beginning to explore and know about themselves.

5. Human and AI collaboration are growing.

More and more of us will get used to the idea of working alongside AI-powered devices and bots in our everyday working lives. Tools are increasingly being developed and allow us to make the best of our human abilities – those that AI can't handle yet – such as creativity, architecture, strategy, and communication skills. Increase them with super-fast computational capabilities powered by large databases that are modified in real-time.

To all of us, that would involve learning new skills, or at least new ways of applying our expertise alongside these modern robotic and software- technologies. IDC estimates that by 2025, 75% of companies should invest in retraining workers to address the skills shortages created by the need to implement AI. This pattern will become increasingly evident across 2020 to the point that, if the company does not invest in AI equipment and preparation, it may be worth thinking how well-positioned they are to develop in the upcoming years.

6. AI increasingly at the "edge."

Much of the AI we're used to communicating with nowadays in our day-to-day lives takes place "in the cloud" – while we search Google or flip through Netflix reviews, sophisticated, data-driven algorithms operate on high-powered processors within remote data centers, with computers in our hands or on our desktops merely serving as a medium for knowledge to flow through.

More than ever, though, as these algorithms get more powerful and able to operate on low- computers, AI takes place at the "bottom," close to the point where data is gathered and used. This model will begin to become more prevalent in 2020 and beyond, making AI-powered predictions a possibility beyond the time and place where super-fast fiber optic and cell networks are available. Custom processors built to do on-the-fly real-time analytics will gradually become part of the infrastructure that we communicate with on-the-fly, and we will eventually be able to do so even though we have patchy or non-existent internet connectivity.

7. AI is gradually used in order to create videos, songs, and games.

Some stuff, even in 2020, is still always best left to men. Anyone who has seen the latest state-- of AI- music, poetry, or storytelling is likely to conclude that the most advanced computers still have a way to go before their performance is as entertaining to us as the best that humans are able to create. Nevertheless, the influence of AI on entertainment media is expected to increase. Last year, we saw Robert De Niro de-aged in front of our eyes with the aid of AI, Martin Scorsese's spectacular The Irishman, and the use of AI to produce entirely new visual effects and trickery is likely to become more popular.

Throughout video games, AI can continue to be used to build competitive, human- enemies for players to battle against, as well as constantly change gameplay and difficulty so that games can continue to be a compelling experience for players at every skill level. So, though AI-generated music might not be everyone's cup of tea, where AI does excel in generating complex soundscapes – think of clever playlists on platforms like Spotify or Google Play that fit tunes so tempo to the mood and rhythm of our daily lives.

8. In cyber defense, AI will become ever more important.

When hacking, phishing, and social manipulation attacks grow more complex, fueled by AI and advanced predictive algorithms, smart technology can play an increasingly important role in shielding us from these alleged intrusions into our lives. AI can be used to identify signals that computer activities or purchases follow habits that are likely to be indicative of malicious behavior and to lift alerts before protections can be broken, and confidential data can be breached.

The roll-of 5G and other super-networking technologies will give companies an incredible opportunity to offer infrastructure in new and creative ways, but it will also theoretically open themselves to more advanced cyber threats. Expenditure on information protection will continue to increase, and those with specific capabilities will be strongly sought-.

9. Many of us are going to communicate with AI, maybe without even realizing it.

Let's face it, given the massive increase in natural-language chatbots in customer care in recent years, none of us is able to know whether we're interacting with a robot or a human. Nevertheless, as the datasets used to train natural language processing algorithms continue to expand, the distinction between humans and machines might become more and more difficult to discern. With the introduction of deep learning and semi-machine learning models such as reinforcement learning, algorithms that aim to suit our speech patterns and derive meaning from our own human language will become more and more capable of fooling us into believing that there is a person at the other end of the conversation. So, while all of us might assume that we would prefer to communicate with a person while searching for either knowledge or assistance, should robots achieve their pledge to become more effective and reliable in answering our requests, that might actually change. Considering the continuing innovation and maturation of technology that powers customer service bots and portals, 2020 might be the first time that many of us have connected with a robot without even knowing it.

10. But even though we don't know it, AI would remember us.

Perhaps even more unsettlingly, the roll-out of facial recognition systems is only expected to accelerate as we step into the next decade. Not only in China (where the government is looking on how to make facial recognition mandatory for access to facilities such as telecom networks and public transport) but around the world. Corporations as well as policymakers are continually engaging in these ways of asking us who we are and understanding our attitudes and behavior. Many pushbacks are coming – this year, San Francisco has become the first big city to prohibit the use of facial recognition technologies by the police and local authorities, and more are expected to suit in 2020. The question of whether people can eventually continue to tolerate this interference into their lives, in exchange for increased protection and comfort, is likely to be a seriously debated topic for the next 12 months.

In summary, research and the advent of Artificial Intelligence will make a significant difference in the next five years. As a result, many enterprises, including e-commerce, retail, and B2B, are leveraging AI in the company sense in order to reap greater benefits.

AI moved beyond robots and science fiction. It's gone far beyond what we might have seen in the past. In reality, it's becoming a norm in the daily life of a common man.

According to Industry Insider, 85% of corporate correspondence will be conducted without human intervention by 2020.

From phone calls to emails and Facebook messages to conversations, both activities are performed by an electronic machine, which is designed to mimic human functions. Artificial intelligence is transforming the general landscape of consumer engagement, but the crucial question to raise is how the future of online and offline business is shifting.

Next, have a look at some of the facts that will help you assess the value of AI in industry.

- More than $300 million in venture capital was spent in AI start-ups in 2014, a rise of 300% over the previous year. (The Bloomberg).

- By 2020, 85% of consumer transactions should be handled without a human being. (The Gartner).

- By the end of 2018, "Customer Personal Assistants" will know consumers by face and voice through networks and alliances (Gartner).

- Artificial intelligence will eliminate 16% of American employment by the end of the decade. (The Forrester).

- 80% of executives agree that artificial intelligence increases the efficiency of employees and generates jobs. (The Story Science).

The application of artificial intelligence in the industry has incredible potential, but for many businessmen, it's very recent and don't realize the value of it yet. When artificial intelligence is gaining traction, both small and large companies are looking forward to reducing costs and keeping ahead of rivals.

Many firms, including fortune 500 businesses, use AI around the board. In case you want to learn how AI will help companies, read the post.

Developing a Personalized Customer interface.

Artificial intelligence allows sales agents to provide consumers with customized experiences. All this is attributed to AI's ability to build more comprehensive frameworks and technologies that simplify business intelligence as well as analytics processes.

Capacity enables showing connections between consumers, previous buying habits, and some other standard behaviors. Transactions of a vast amount will be evaluated on a regular basis in order to deliver deals to a single client.

Artificial Intelligence can help e-commerce firms overcome market problems with timely intelligence. This will allow the sales rep to recognize the commodity that consumers will be most likely to purchase. For example, once they speak with a prospective customer, they would be well aware of what they need and deliver the product effectively.

Writing Stories from Algorithms.

Story telling has also been a tool for companies in order to target consumers. Writing stories from available data can be a lot easier than writing a traditional story. The traditional myths, however, distorted the basis behind the inference.

Nowadays, businesses are engaging in data monetization using the Natural Language Generation program in order to write data material automatically. This would not have been possible for a poor citizen to write without adequate tools. Data-driven stories are more focused on the wants and desires of future buyers, leading to more purchases across stories.

Better Customer Service and Support.

Chatbots will be the next service agent able to provide assistance to consumers. Instead of digging for the answers to your questions, just ask the chatbot to get the answers and support your needs. In fact, the bot must also decide whether to precede the higher management question or grant a reservation.

The whole cycle of customer service is going to ramp up. Without any doubt, there would be less risk of any human error, and the pace of the help process would definitely save time. In addition, information can be created by chatting with the chatbot instead of reading posts, the FAQ tab, and the segment.

Differentiate Brand with Human Concierge.

Premium brands will be able to set them apart by delivering a real person on the call, either by phone or by chat. Many people would like to listen to a human voice instead of an artificial machine voice. The human touch would then be a perfect way to overpower a dumb bot.

Artificial intelligence technologies are currently providing new ways for the company to stand out. There may be no robots that can keep up with people, or have the potential to act like them, but as time progresses, they're more practical and changing the market scenario.

Marketing and Advertising.

New and creative techniques have modified the way marketing and advertisement have been done. For instance, you can show commercials for goods or services of your choice without being asked. It's all because of the artificial intelligence that most corporations have embraced. Identify your previous searches and show the results based on your background.

Artificial intelligence is also a method of marketing goods or services in a different way. By really letting the consumer know, businesses will force their goods to buy. Using artificial intelligence, advertisers are able to simplify lots of daily tasks, collect critical data, and spend time deciding ways to increase customer loyalty as well as sales.

Automation of Manual Operations.

The rise in technology has contributed to the outsourcing of jobs. Machines such as automobiles, home appliances, and factory robotics have displaced human labor, therefore saving a lot of energy. For comparison, advanced robots are capable of working alongside humans in factories.

MIT Economist, David Autor, sees the emergence of a new age of globalization, where the division of labor is not classified as white-collar VS blue-collar, but as routine vs. non-routine work.

Such advanced systems will work 24 hours a day, 365 days a year, without the need for coffee breaks. For example, an investment bank can use Artificial Intelligence to simplify human work by gathering data from different sources and doing an analysis to determine the viability of the business.

Do Not Go Yet; One Last Thing to Do

If you enjoyed this book or found it useful, I'd be very grateful if you'd post a short review on it. Your support does make a difference, and I read all the reviews personally so I can get your feedback and make this book even better.

Thanks again for your support!